T0137577

NATION'S HISTORICAL SENSE AND ECCLESIALITY FOR LIFE

Nationalistic Church Witness of Catholicity

Junes Almodiel

Order this book online at www.trafford.com
or email orders@trafford.com

Most Trafford titles are also available at major online book retailers.

Printed in the United States of America.

ISBN: 978-1-4269-5971-4 (sc)
ISBN: 978-1-4269-5970-7 (hc)
ISBN: 978-1-4269-5969-1 (e)

Library of Congress Control Number: 2011910697

Trafford rev. 07/05/2011

 www.trafford.com

North America & international
toll-free: 1 888 232 4444 (USA & Canada)
phone: 250 383 6864 ♦ fax: 812 355 4082

CONTENTS

Preface

I am grateful to Reverend Fr. Apolonio Ranche, who taught ecclesiastical history and helped me to discover what I am passionate about. I am also thankful to my classmates during those years of learning at Saint Andrew's Theological Seminary. I am grateful that Bishop Gregorio de los Reyes, son of Bishop Isabelo de los Reyes Jr. and grandson of the cofounder of Iglesia Filipina Independiente, Isabelo de los Reyes Sr., was my bishop during my first year in parish work. I dedicate this work to them and to those who love and gave their support to the Church IFI.

The purpose of this writing is to share some religious perspective that is basically coming from the point of view of the Christian believers of the nationalistic Church who organized themselves as part of a freedom movement after more than three hundred years of the colonial and imperial eras. Though my motive is to share some thoughts about this nationalist Church, the primary reason for the narrative is to unburden the feelings from my heart regarding the historical and nationalistic Iglesia Filipina Independiente (IFI), or Philippine Independent Church (PIC). It is known as a product of the people's initiative for freedom and independence, popularly known as Aglipayan (after the name of its first head bishop, Gregorio Aglipay). IFI or PIC is also known as Filipinista—as opposed to Romanista (Romanist) and Americanista (Americanist).

A burden in my heart caused me to reflect about IFI—thoughts that I felt needed to be shared that may serve as instruments to contribute thoughts, ideas, concepts, or stories to serve life for all. The Filipino people—with their learning past—can be part of shaping the community of people in the light of the nation's historical heritage and may point to Christian teachings or Gospel that can make people realize the importance of God's purpose in the Gospel relevant to people's struggle in pursuit of peace, justice, and fairness. The IFI happened to be one perfect example of the expression.

Being the "only living, tangible result" and the "crowning glory" of freedom initiative and struggle for independence, the IFI shared the banner of respect for human dignity and justice rooted in pro life/people Christian messages (as opposed to "spirit after death and heaven only" kind of Christianity). It is right to say that the depth of anti-colonialism or anti-imperialism as reaction and revolution are defined not in terms of military might by the defenders against the invader who displayed power over the meek and weak humans. Instead, this is about exercising the revealing design that points to humans' Designer.[1] This is also to show the vulnerability of the "winner" in their regrettable pro-market drive in manipulating the chances in the world. IFI must tell her story.

Common Filipinos today need to be awakened from being detached from their heart and sense of history and being naïve as victim of mis-education regarding their nation's state projected by pro-imperialists that still affect the way they think. The imperialists' influence definitely affected the way they judge, treat, or view things. A perfect example is how the Filipino IFI is regarded by Filipinos—instead of treasuring this historical Church to make sense of Christian religion away from "end time" enthusiasm of pro-imperialist Fundamentalists, many Filipinos still idolized the imperialists' greatness or capability that made them ashamed of their own historical achievement. They ridicule the nationalistic IFI for their colonial mentality—even though the Church is one concrete result of human endeavor in manifesting the good creature.

In careful thinking, things like Filipino history should be treated justly due to the fact that this is one raw material to see the depth revealing of the capability of human beings (that even though brown Filipino by race) he has meaningful response to his own situation and call of his own time. Their normal responses in history are their honest display of being human in submission to the nature that human became human, following the order he/she is expected to behave according to the nature or characteristic design reflecting his Designer's wisdom and greatness. Historical evidence—its importance and actuality in man's struggle for freedom and pursuit of justice for lasting peace—must be treated as sacred. Truly there is transcendental evidence, breathed by God, in man, who truly understood life the moment he is willing to die for it.

Filipino history and struggle in the imperial era were part of the assertion of the Filipino people's right to be treated equally and to coexist in the world with mutual respect, allowing them to develop and grow themselves, discover the full potential of their human race, contribute to the common good as people of the world to stand as humans and not enablers of the weaknesses of the unjust, be saved and detached from offensive acts, and build the sanctuary of race appropriate to the visions and ideals of the nation's founders and according to the purpose of God to the benefit of "living being" as designed for here and now and so hereafter. As shown in the pages of history, Filipinos demanded freedom to restore their ability to be friends again with other neighboring countries and races, friendships they enjoyed before the coming of Spaniards. American authors recognized this fact by stating that when Ferdinand Magellan discovered the islands in 1521, he "found a literate population linked by trade ties to India, Japan, and China."[2]

Challenges for the Christian Church today are seen in the works of religious isms. They seem connected to the claims of the imperialists. Literalism, Bible-ism, fundamentalism, and dogmatism of the religion of colonial and imperial agendas are not the purpose of God. Above all, it is not the purpose of God to derail the mind of the oppressed and oppressors, avoiding the pro-life and pro people Christianity and the purpose of Jesus Christ for the salvation of both sides from making the pro life/people and the Gospel away from being the center stage of Christian living. Biblical messages can be missed by absolute literalism—and they can be a place of abusing the scripture, playing with ignorance as the result of "Bible only" literalism. Abuse in the sense that they can stop being literal if the Church wanted to in many areas (selectively), according to fundamentalist nature in pleasing the giant ruler of the world, but she is hijacked at the same time to make "divine sanction" of sustaining the rule. Selectively literal depends on what imperial power they wanted to please. Serving one political party's agenda against the pro-life/people purpose of God? God must be "displaced"—a fact that must not be ignored.

I
Introduction

What made people—or Filipinos in particular—detached or disconnected from their historical sense, and seemingly ashamed of their own history? The "education" in history, by those who are aware of the reason called it "miseducation" of Filipino people. This is because the dominant and reigning religious and political sectors are still strongly maintaining the status quo over the rightful agent of the ultimate pro-Filipino education. Ruling religious or political sectors may be offended by the philosophies and pro-Filipino ideals by our Filipino patriots in history, as they still sold out to the claims and methods of the religious institutions defensively and anticipating against what Filipinos are fighting for. The nation's political leadership seems to be trying to please the giant who may have the total capacity to terrorize the whole race or nation by its complete killing machine. Truly "liberating education" is overpowered by the propaganda machine of the pro-imperialist institutions. The enlightening pro masses or people in history to free the nation from worshipping the "superior" is still subject to our honest endeavor.

Pointing out the roadblocks and hindrances of the human truth displayed in history must be our task to free the honest truth to serve life and people. Historical sense should make sense to the lives of people; we should be asking why things cannot succeed. With sincere hearts and intentions, we bring basic challenges, issues, and concerns to our attention as good starting tools for the discussion of what we thought will lead us toward what is pleasing to the Lord of Justice and the Prince of Peace.

Real *Filipino history* makes a big deal of how we see the achievements of the past. Real truth and history should find alternatives to propaganda and myth-making by pro-foreign authors. This should show that the spirit of struggle for freedom cannot be stopped by the intimidating military might and the work of injustices. The Iglesia Filipina Independiente (IFI) is one example of the continuation of the unstoppable spirit of struggle in pursuing justice. IFI held that the end of Filipino struggle is not determined by the power of the enemy's weapons, but by the moral judgment in the innermost human mind. This aspect should not be excluded in building up a community. Real Christianity is not stuck with religious dogmatism and claims as captivating instruments. It is Christianity of God's love for all people and races, according to the witnesses of the historically grounded nationalistic Church. It is one freeing agent for life.

Reactions to injustices were exercised by the same people who understood the message of God's love for all people; therefore, the significance of "real and honest history" must be respected. The function of history should be protected from disrespect for somebody's rigid selfish intention. Should this be made serving as an instrument to see God's design in humans that leads to glorifying

God—the Designer manifested in human history? Honestly, we cannot call it with another word, but as actual exercise and action of God's design in man responding to the real situations created by man. Indeed, human design must shape history and the actuality of it must be protected. Historians must act as "scene protectors" until truth and justice is served. By that is seen "the beauty of God's total order, designed, as it is, according to the laws of His justice."[3] History should serve as an instrument to understand life, people, human events, and Creation. "Real history" will serve as an instrument to point out the final greatness and beauty of God. Man is only following the order designed of his nature—and reveals the beauty of the Creator. Truth should be liberated and celebrated—with God and for God.

There are reasons why man cannot recognize the divine attributes evident in human normalcy displayed in history is by suppression of honest education for propaganda purpose by historians subservient to imperialists—and by religious institutions aiming to gain protections from imperial power pinning the name of God to the imperialist action, though exercising the opposite. The supposedly freeing Church is seemingly trapped to confusion; Filipino responses against inequality are called "evil" by them. Indeed, the ability to identify the enemy of God's purpose in life is clouded.

The IFI Church is now recognized by Filipino historians as "the only living and tangible result of the (Filipino) Revolution."[4] So, pursuing the spirit of Filipino struggle in religious expression, the historic and nationalistic IFI deserved to have rightful place in the national and community building (as part of history, and that is if we people still have the capacity to see the sanctity of real honest human and true to his conscience, moral law and judgment, or feeling responding to the reality of his world.

Filipino revolutionaries also reflected that faith in God helped their courage to fight for freedom; that faith also served as a vehicle for historical exercise. The heartbeat of national fathers (heroes) led to responding in achieving the new condition away from cruel evil imperialism/colonialism of their time. Injustice is revealed and steps of its removal are the normal response by humans. Indeed, Filipinos in history reflect the divine—and human—design. Praise to His greatness.

Love for God is in action and the love of God is revealed as they continued aspiring for freedom, respect, and independence. So, when America's 1902 empire was proclaimed by its president as the "winner" in the Philippines, a new way—a religious non-violent Christian movement—was founded. IFI served as a new vehicle for the new face of the same aspiration nationwide. Sustained by Christian spirit and Biblical teachings on God's love for all, it was strengthened by the "fatherhood of God and the brotherhood of all people."[5] Reflecting the depth of freedom, national justice, love, and brotherhood are summed up in the theme "Kingdom of God" that should be felt by our close and intimate relationship with God, sustained by the desire of Christian hearts. Real history shows beyond a person's name, date, and event—it is a display of moral responsibility.

Issues of *human conduct* and *moral responsibility* must be displayed in the record of history so that by reading them we may ask 'is it the work of a human or a beast?' Human action comes when the actual reality of life touches us humans. With honest and rightful (Godly and humanly) motives, we all know that we should exercise our God's gift of freedom and powerful capability to defend and promote human lives. As people with history and experience in reality, we took pain to reflect on things about the sanctity of human life. The IFI Epistle (initial teachings) said "Our painful separation (from Rome) is based on sound reason and above all on the natural need to protect our rights and our national dignity."[6] This reveals the moral issue of the time in which the nationalist Church is the natural outcome of the human response with a learned past. The evil of 1902 by racists building of imperialism for market was real and felt by Filipinos. The response to consider the alternative, embracive, inclusive, and liberating love of God became their ultimate option.

This should serve as the guiding light for the darkness caused by the new ruler connived by the ally foreigner's religion. Filipinos in history saw the "light of the world" (Jesus) must be visible and real to their darkened world. Thus, a nationalistic Church is embraced by people of historical sense as a vehicle for liberty (under God's will, truth, and light). Moral sense causing the Church to be found as one result of the heartbeat of humans must cause the Church of Christ to be pro-people and sensitive to what is learned from the past. With a Christian lens, these Filipinos saw the ruinous, devilish darkness done to their nation. It ends in the power of God's love, justice, and liberating truth, played in the struggle for life. Lies, falsehoods, or deceptions in history and in retelling "history" are manifestations of the offended, but they lost the capacity to stand what represents Jesus and His teachings. These must come to end as the promises of Christian spirit begin to be fulfilled.

At that time, Vatican and Papal-centered Catholicism—being one with an instrument of the market-driven capitalist's imperialism—

is surely the cause of the birth of religious nationalism. It is one natural outcome—good, human, and divinely revealing. Since the beginning of revolutionary operations, Filipinos have demonstrated their philosophies and religious beliefs. Not stuck to prove their bravery, they revealed their willingness to die for freedom, equality, and human dignity. Struggle was embraced—not because of mental religious doctrines—but by inherently built-in moral judgment and sense of human responsibility in them. In this, there is no evolutionary or biological explanation; hence, it points to the divine.

Filipino *history writers* cause an honest historian to consider *rewriting* their history after myth making. We were taught that to be fully human, we must study our own history. It's a good thought, right? Who wrote that Filipino and IFI history? The reality requires one to be so responsible in learning to reclaim the lost historical sense, heritage, and sense of nationalism. How good was it to think that all the ability and capability is to be used in serving the truth that reveals the absolute good—and that points to something great. But sadly, in the kingdom of imperialism, historical truth (actuality) cannot serve the agenda of the powerful (imperialist) ruler. History must be censored in the interests of the empire's propaganda machine—and to serve its policy.

Responsible ones must know the history, motives, and agendas of the authors. Filipino historian Pedro Gagelonia (University of Santo Tomas, UST) said "The founding of the PIC (or IFI), to the knowledge of the ordinary student of history, is shrouded with mystery. This is due to the fact that the majority of our historians choose to relegate almost to obscurity the role played by the PIC in our nation building."[7] Servants of foreign agendas and antagonists to the Filipino nationalist movement wrote "propaganda history" to please their "lord" with their service to foreign institutions (political or religious). Renato Constantino wrote:

> All nations, including the USA, are proud of their revolutions, because revolutions signify a drastic and basic change in their national lives achieved by the people themselves for their own interest. We stand out as an exception, for our Revolution seems detached from our lives. It is because, from the beginning, there was an attempt to downgrade it and to misrepresent its legitimate goals in order to make the climate safe for the further propagation of myth. This myth was further developed by the American historical version of the period, fostered by historical propagandists, strengthened by our uncritical acceptance of this version of history, and elaborated by various misconceptions that emanated from this acceptance.[8]

So we learned myths in the past, but not complete history. One pro-foreign historian and author may play with his *yes* and *no* in serving the trapped rulers (for justification or the desired global position for control and market), but the result of it all boils down to the realization that man and woman ought not to be naïve in laziness and carelessness. They could indirectly empower this and sustain that which is selfish or ungodly. Motives like that cannot represent Christ's teachings. God can use something to point that out one day. Effort is crucial to "enter the narrow gate" for the truth and for the glory of God.

I am grateful to Filipino authors like Agoncillo, Constantino, Scott, and Gagelonia who faced the challenge and recognized the need for a new perspective for truth that must be saved from the attempt to downgrade and misrepresent the legitimate goals of freedom's struggle in the pages of history. To be able to narrate the true spirit of history for the sake of truth, we can be proud of our very own people. Indeed, history may serve as a revealing agent to understand the character of Filipino people in history—only to know that we all deserve the same respect (with heart, mind, and strength). Honesty of historians is crucial to serving the truth. We must see honesty and truth serving for human good and for human life. Truth that glorifies and reflects the beauty of God (differed from the father of lies, Jn 8:44) is in the hand of both writer and the choice of the reader. It is sad to say that history writing also became a vehicle for deceptions and lies to serve the market-driven agenda of economic imperialism. The result of the materialism, consumerism, and the exploitation of natural resources (served by pro-imperialist history making) is done to the "weak" people.

Our *earth stewardship* and global warming is one concern that every individual should have today. Environmental situations may need us to revisit the motives of 1898 imperialist man's enthusiasm for "market for surplus product" as the very reason of US Republican imperialism that finally gained "success" in 1902 after the Filipino-American War. That was where and when America achieved the title "world power." Our climate change today seems to be the result of the culture brought by materialist and capitalist empire after a hundred years of making and influencing materialism to the simple God-fearing people. We may be addicted and reach the point of no return where it consumes and destroys us. We got a judgment of our conduct by supplanting the old culture of simplicity and their "worship" to nature into the culture of progressive consumerism to keep capitalist's company exploiting it.

It turns out that the Filipino resistance from 1899 to 1902—and the Anti-Imperialist League in America against the US invasion of the Philippines for implementing the global commercial and materialist ambition—served as the right action. It was not only good for the Philippines, but also for the earth's environment. It was not only good for Filipino, but also for humanity and the victims of capitalist/consumerist cultural ruins and territorial chaos. It tells something about respecting the earth and all humankind and races—as "all human are created equal."

Now imperialist and materialist success is deeply rooted to the way of life that is now hard to adjust to according to the demand based on climate change or global warming. Here, it must be said, is one potential for the powerful to ignore its truth because of the embarrassment that it would bring to the arrogant. It may create some drastic move to save face. It may bring hope for events to take place for the self-centered or the chance to avert the attention. It could also passively use this as another opportunity for commercial gain to satisfy the spirit of the commercial opportunist. This must be the time that prideful arrogance must serve honestly and truthfully for life that humans ought to serve in the first place.

When the cry of Filipinos for human dignity is ignored for the sake of expansionist isms that disrespect other's religious concepts— that in effect ruined the sanctuary of their own identity and race —the ways of God is supplanted. We should "seek His kingdom first and all these things shall be given unto us." Addiction to success over others leads to chaos, but there is something for lasting peace and life that is the real spirit of the Christian mission. Position, politics, power, and prestige are already established where materialists are. These should be used—perhaps there is no other alternative—to submit to this thought: "Whoever wants to become great among you must be your servant and whoever wants to be first must be slave of all." (Mk 10:43–44).

The real situation today may force us to embrace the way of life taught by Jesus that is friendly to the environment—and not craving wealth, "worship of Mammon," or aiming for wealth with no satisfaction. The worship for God of love, life, and fairness must be lifted up. We know that man can do ruinous acts for wealth if we do not watch. Out of the darkness, there is the founding of pro-people IFI to serve as a vehicle of liberating truth of God that is pro-life/people instead of pro-Mammon/wealth.

Since its founding, the challenge for IFI/PIC is how to keep its spirit—and to pass to the next generation the rich heritage of the Church to reach to its deeper understanding without being affected by the sectarian and pro-imperialist *bully* pulpit that surrounded her. Because of a lack of resources, the members of this Church tend to forget the wisdom that should be sustained. They tend to believe what is seen in the nature of surrounding sects that Church is about a contest of the capacity to assert their own *truth and claims*. There is a tendency to leave the fact that IFI is in strategic position to make sense of Christianity to help discover the pro-people shape of ecclesiality (from the word ecclesia or Iglesia—church) for all people of the world to see. By its historical sense, it will bring the banner of the Light of the world (Christ) for the darkness done by the worship of wealth.

One aim of this book is that all historically grounded nationalistic Churches (like IFI) must not be pushed to persecution. All people of the world have nations to love, national history to cherish, and love for God. It must not be seen as the opposite—we are not talking about jingoism over nationalism. Lovers of respect and justice for his own nation and its history, the name of God should not appear as the enemy, offensive, or deceptive. His name should not be put in vain. Humans cry for love and respect. In the nationalistic Church, God is the answer.

In Christ's pro-life teachings, we hope to see Christian values as an alternative to the racist greed of chance or things that bring chaos, hatred, and insecurity that ruin human order and life. Church is *not* an agent to disconnect people's love for freedom and God. The work of the Church and its historical sensitivity should be counted (with her Kingdom work) for the brotherhood of all (in Christ) under God's fatherhood. Nationalist Church products of history are a treasure for building life and must be defended and sustained.

On Historical Sense and Ecclesiality

Spanish philosopher Ortega y Gasset mentioned "historical sense." Church historian John E. Booty wrote:

> If we ignore history, we deteriorate, becoming less than fully human. If we refuse to study the past, we abdicate from the power and authority, which we rightly possess over the historical forces that impinged upon us, and we are in grave

danger of being led like dumb oxen into the future. There are strong tendencies within us to conform to the dominant intellectual, moral, and cultural trends of the present age, without thought, without criticism, and without control.[9]

Gasset's "historical sense" is the "sense" by which we perceive the past. Traveling away from ourselves into that past, we will gain the necessary perspective on the present. If we exercise this sense, we will gain the leverage needed to break away from the forces who seek to control us, and we will regain our lost humanity. We will also be better prepared to move creatively into the future.[10]

To conform to something without critical thinking empowers those who seek to control us. So our weakness instilled upon us by imperialist "educator" propagandists is going to be a stronghold for them against us. We become less human and dumb if we only practice submission to those who forced their claims as the "only civilized and superior" ones over others or us.

Filipino national hero Dr. Jose P. Rizal taught that "anyone who does not look back where he came from, he cannot reach to his vision goal," (*ang hindi lilingon sa pinanggalingan ay hindi makakarating sa parorounan*). I believed that this is not without deeper meaning. For this purpose, I should reflect that our historical lessons from the past experiences, teachings of the founding fathers (heroes) who fought for our future, their philosophies or principles, community codes, reasons of blood compacts with other "friendly" race, rules, and laws that served them right, reasons of their rebellions against the evil invaders, their developed civilization, life and blood of patriots, etc. should not be forgotten. Instead, these should serve as instruments to gain back the Filipino confidence, humanity, pride, dignity, sense of nationalism, and self-respect. Consider these as light and be counted for our purpose in life toward lasting peace of a wider world community. How "deserving of pity" for a man to run just because others were running, without understanding why he should run and imitate others away from his own roots, historical foundation, identity, humanness, uniqueness, and purpose.

"Go with the flow" people are often instruments or enablers of somebody's selfish agenda against them. Is it because the intimidation of the imperialist winner is so powerful? No, cowardice that empowers those powers of injustice and evil didn't represent God's design in them. It seems that God is not so great with that kind of nature. Empty minds, naiveté, and callousness displayed by the victim or the victimizer may bring down our belief in God and our being.

Our bloody past and struggle for freedom against evils and injustices should draw the identity that builds and sustains our honor and dignity. We have the roots, history, philosophy, and understanding of the sanctity of life. The pro-imperialists made Filipinos believe that their history was shameful. Filipinos are now conditioned to think with feelings of inferiority. Religious sects—as allies of the imperialists—showed a double standard. They were too cowardly to oppose what is offensive to the inclusive love of God, irrelevant religion, haven of hypocrisy, and selfishness.

Our continued call to unity aims to restore, rescue, or reclaim the good image of the Church of Christ that must represent the Creator and His teachings in Christ. If the church of *conquistadores* or imperialists is trapped to serve the *inequality* of humans with their religious dogmatism or claims (where they can still feel good amid darkness) subservient to their "idol" grabber of power and imperialists isms, justifying it with their version of interpretation of the their "gospel"—see the difference in historical Churches like IFI (with the Gospel of brotherhood of all people)—came out from human cry for freedom and respect for human dignity, there is freedom to proclaim God's beautiful purpose and His truth that blesses the whole humanity—and the total man (with spirit, heart, mind, soul, flesh, and emotion) and not to deceive people by saying "spirit and heaven only." If the pro-imperialist Church "lost its ethics because of its identification of Christianity with modern culture of capitalism" (said Rosemary Radford Ruether, theologian), the struggle for freedom and human dignity has "transcendental overtones" (using the word of theologian Wilfred Smith). God's truth has historical dimensions. He is seen as actively involved in human history, the human struggle for freedom, justice, respect, equality, and love.

The usefulness of the Church for the purposes of God should be honest, visible, and real. We do not intend to put away religious dogmas, doctrines, practices, promises of life after death, eternity, or heaven, but these should not cover up the shocking and ugly actions of the colonizers or imperialists against the weak. These biblical terms that the pro-imperialist Church can play with (as they did) lead people to focus on heaven and not the reality of occupation and evil on earth, and the devastation and mistrust that it brings.

People with history may say that "we witnessed the reality of powerful evil (the work of Satan manifested in man with a callous heart and telling lies) seen in the death of the helpless and weak, reflecting the worship of material and advancement of technology or weaponry. Words must be voiced that loving God is the opposite of it. Time is precious and is to be used for the liberating Truth of God. IFI was born in the reality and situation that God's goodness about how to relate to other people must be pointed out as Jesus voiced the Kingdom of God in the midst of Caesar's—not to crusade for anti-race, person, or country, but against the conduct by imperialists, we raise Christ's concept of love is appropriate enough to be celebrated. In IFI Epistles, *love* is taught to include the enemy because we have faith in humans. This is not to make enemies clap their hands, but it is a revolutionary concept for the Kingdom of God.

The ignorance of enslaved Filipino people is the enemy for saving them from chains. The Bible said, "My people are destroyed for the lack of knowledge" (Hosea 4:6). To awaken the Filipino people, national hero Dr. Jose Rizal wrote *Noli Me Tangere* (Touch Me Not). About this, Trinidad H. Pardo de Tavera said, "The prestige which the friars had enjoyed, and which was based only on the ignorance of the masses." He proved that the passage is right. Ignorance by choice or by deception by pro-imperialist educators seems empowered by naiveté and a "don't care" attitude. Honest and correct knowledge—witnessed by the learned man in history—is strength in the rightful purpose away from being less than fully human. We have reasons to cry out to God to be with us for the issue of life and respect for human dignity. Filipino ideals, thoughts, and principles that came out after their experience in history, manifests (not enemy) the normal human nature that is in us. It sustains our humanness as we continue to give lights to all. It causes us to reflect upon the beauty of the liberating purpose of God. Maybe the world is pushed to deterioration and ending (as what the fundamentalist wants you to think as fundamental truth to anticipate the promised rapture) by the ways of wasteful materialist and consumerist culture, but our calling for moral responsibility still is "hate what is evil, cling to what is good" (Rm. 12:9) still truth to bear and not obsolete in our time.

A continuation of freedom's voice, IFI became one strategic vehicle for the great and lasting purpose. IFI's Bishop Delfin M. Callao Sr. (Diocese of Davao), named as "People's Bishop," taught that before the death of Jose Rizal in his farewell letter, Rizal said that there is hope, the "dawn for light" is coming. Callao said that the IFI was the only living product of history that came out of the national revolution that became a religious home for nationalists.

After those fallen movements (such as the Propaganda movement, Katipunero-KKK, Revolutionary government), IFI is exercising with historical sense and held freedom as a gift from God, is appropriate to be that "dawning light." All the patriots were in the IFI movement, but the patriots embraced the *real* light of the world and salvation from the chain of manmade darkness. Christ was centered in the worship of the IFI. Reflecting Christ's light is the actual nature of the Church. This is not for the destructing arrogance so that the claims will lead the Church away from God. The torch of light landed upon IFI's lap there is no choice but to lift it up as light for all people and races. Our obligation and mission in baptismal covenant is to work with those in the right position to serve the Kingdom of God.

As Christians, we say Church/message/the Christ. This can mean IFI/respect-justice-freedom-love-brotherhood/Light (see John 1: 4–9; 8:12). It is correct in theological thinking to say that this light is Christ's by the Church—acting as reflection and extension of Jesus. The light of the world is incarnated by the freed, learned, educated new men. This became the motivating factor for the IFI members that put so much respect for the IFI Church. They sustained and protected it as God's gift for the present time and for the time to come. God's will is grounded in the field where humans spilled the blood and built life's destiny. IFI represents someone coming from the effects of ruining darkness must speak up about the pain of darkness for the purpose of embracing the light of life's journey.

IFI as the People's Religious Expression

Filipino historians stood for the "sanctity of actuality." They claimed that the Spanish soldiers were defeated by Filipinos in revolution. Dr. Manolo Vaño (of IFI and U.P., Cebu) corrected Bp. Vic Esclamado, in his letter.

> I heard you Rt. Reverend saying that we were defeated, as if the struggle for freedom by the Filipino simply ended in futility. As a matter of fact, we defeated the Spaniards in 1898, but before the Filipino-American war started in Feb. 1899, the Vatican brought together American and Spanish representatives on Dec. 10, 1898, in order to overpower the Filipinos ... Nevertheless, my disagreement with you on this one point—I don't accept we were defeated ...[11]

The said defeat is seen when Spaniards and friars (Romanist priests)—after years of Filipino revolution against Spaniards—were confined inside the walled city of Manila. They waited for aid and troops from Spain that didn't come. The Filipino's (supposed) ally—America—was in Manila Bay waiting for more troops to come. Expansionist Americans leaders had a hidden plan to keep the Philippines for their global agenda.

The Declaration of Philippine Independence took place on June 12, 1898, by Filipinos led by Emilio Aguinaldo in Cavite. After this, Filipinos thought that Americans—revealing their actual intentions to take the Philippines from Spain—had no legal way to take place. Instead, they should respect the infant independent Filipino republic—they struggled for almost four hundred years against the cruelty of Spaniards, friars, and foreign rulers. But American expansionists desired to keep the Philippines, affirmed by the 1898 Treaty of Paris between America and Spain. Therefore, three years of Filipino-American war took place and the infant Filipino nation lost its newly proclaimed independence. The war halted in 1902, but non-violent expression of freedom continued and also suffered.

There were certain patterns in Filipino history: When their "hope" person or group died, a new one was born. When the Gom-Bur-Za (Fathers Gomez, Burgos, and Zamora) died, they founded the Propaganda movement. When Dr. Jose Rizal (Filipinos hoped that he would lead them out of the darkness of injustice) got arrested, they founded a secrete association called Katipunan or KKK (should not be mistaken for Ku Klux Klan in USA). The Filipino KKK stands for *Kataastaasan, Kagalanggalangan, Katipunan ng anak ng Bayan* (Highest, Most Respectable Society of the Sons of the People). In short, Katipunan is the revolutionary movement for freedom and independence. When the three men of Propaganda died in 1896, the Philippine Revolution started and Aguinaldo became well known. The revolution continued the cause of freedom through the Philippine government headed by Emilio Aguinaldo. When the

Philippine government was finally crushed by the Americans in 1902, the IFI (in which Aguinaldo is a member) was born.

In the midst of the mighty powerful imperialists, the new Filipino hope was the God of the Church. IFI was a Church carrying the Filipino cause with a religious lens that viewed freedom and respect for human dignity as the purpose of God in humanity. They looked at God—in the historical sense—as revealing part of His greatness.

In the imperialist era, Renato Constantino stated that, while advocacy for independence is prohibited, the "strong nationalist sentiments of the people had to find expression in ostensibly non-political areas ... by the Philippine Independent Church (PIC)."[12] As already said, Teodoro Agoncillo stated that PIC is "the only living and tangible result of the Revolution."[13] Other names for IFI like Filipino Catholic or Independiente, plus another name like Filipinista (Filipinist) as opposed to Romanista (Romanist))—shows the connection of the movement to the Filipino cause. "Independent" connotes freedom. In the Tagalog region, they call it *Simbahang Malaya* (independent or freed church). The truth of this is strongly supported by early documents of the IFI, which we deal later.

The Church was viewed as the remaining Filipino treasure and light bearer for future life. In the eyes of IFI Filipinos, Christianity is a vehicle for God's love and brotherhood of all in God with its message for life. The Romanists seem to project the Church as if Christianity is a popularity contest. The number should be drawn by all means to win the competition. This is an offensive regard to the real spirit of Christianity and an assault to the human's revealing nature manifested in struggle and marks of history. It seems that the sentiment for human respect doesn't count.

Years after its founding, IFI experienced the sad reality caused by the unified actions of two foreign institutions: American politics and Romanist religion against this nationwide religious nationalist movement; but some thinkers respected the IFI Church as "the right church for the pro-people struggle"[14]. IFI's presence in history also served as the living religious proof and symbol of the fulfillment of the first Philippine government's clear intention to have Filipino-Catholic (not Roman)-Independent-Christian Philippines. Kenneth Latourette said that the PIC/IFI is "the child of Filipino nationalism."[15]

As we study IFI, we hope to see (or share to shape) that the nationalistic Church may serve as sharer of ecclesiality true to God's design. The world will view history as a result of that *order* in which the Church must reveal or reflect the aspects and facts that point to God's glorification. The truth is that if man is only honest to himself (no denying factors involved), he will respond to his reality and situation according to the function of his mind, heart, emotion, will, and conscience. It will not have (celebrated) naiveté, but will be wise with his/her built-in moral judgment—in his/her innermost being able to see the right from wrong. Indeed, it is a manifestation of God's greatness. Opponents bullied IFI as an "imitation" to the Romanist Church, but the two are like oppressed and oppressor. Nationalistic IFI's reason is not for imitation; real history can mirror the beauty of God—and so can the IFI. The IFI should not throw practices and divine traditions passed on by the Apostles to the early Church, to the Greek Church, etc. The historical IFI is one mark of respectable humankind that does not deny the ultimate good, great, (as St. Augustine's) "wisdom of their Designer."[16]

II
The Root of a Nation's Historical Sense

As a result of the claim, teaching, or doctrine of the Romanist Church, some Filipino Romanists ridiculed the IFIs. They said, "We have this true and original church. Why should we consider the other?" We don't need to have another church (as what Filipinos thought for more than three hundred years under monarchial/friar period). If Christianity is all about doctrines, dogma, and claims—nothing to do with actuality of human actions affecting people—then religion is just for religion and not a blessing for life. Reaction to injustice and selfish racism are realities that should shape how we see things. Revolution against injustice absolutely counts in our response to life. In this chapter, we aim to see factors that became the framework of events in history. They caused the Filipino race to surface as it played in the fields to understand life as it engaged in related actualities. One factor that changed the life of the Filipino society was the introduction of colonial government.

Filipinos were not coming from caves when Spaniards taught their ways, but the natives had their own established customs and social life. The Philippines was dotted with independent village-states called *barangay*. Each barangay had its own barangay government ruled by the head of the village (Datu). This ruling Datu exercised the executive, legislative, and judicial powers. Not to act independently, they had a council of elders to give advice on serious matters. Some barangays formed confederations for protection against common enemies. The other reason was marriage of a prince (lakan) to the other barangay's princess (lakambini). Baranganic relations sometimes formed because of trade. They had written laws and judicial procedures, religion, music, language, writings, literature, and trade relations with other countries.[17]

We don't need to detail how the early Filipinos enjoyed trade with India, China, and Japan. Luis Francia wrote that the Philippines has pre-colonial ports that served the world trade. "Butuan (Mindanao) was one of the most active, probably the center of trade and commerce in the islands during the eleventh century."[18] The evolving civilization came into disturbance when the Spaniards arrived.

Under the Banner of Patronato Real Español

In AD 1564, the Philippines became under the rule of Patronato Real. The Roman Catholic Pope gave ultimate religious authority to the Spanish king (monarch) through Patronato Real Español. This was about headship of the Church by the Royal Patron. When Manila was created as one of Roman Catholic dioceses on February 6, 1578, the Papal Bull decreed, "We grant to the same King Philip, power to assign, increase, extend, lessen, and otherwise change the bounds therein. Moreover, we reserve, grant and assign forever to the king the right of patronage of the Church over the Church in Manila." [19]

The spread of Christianity became the primary justification of the territorial interest of the patron and had the final say to determine the number of Church mission territories and to approve the assignment of missionaries. How was this implemented?

The Encomienda system of government was adapted in all Spanish colonies. The Encomendero (from the word "to entrust") was charged to rule the natives within the specific geographic area. The primary function was to take the rule of king of the village; he represented the role or delivered the task of the monarch as Royal Patron. He was supposed to instruct the natives with Catholic faith and Castilian tongue; he had given the power to collect tribute (tax) for the sustenance and implementation of his tasks. The tribute furnished the revenue for expenses for the missionaries imparting the Catholic doctrine and managing the encomienda. It provided the encomendero and his family their means of living. The movement of the natives was regulated to ensure a steady supply of labor and the prompt collection of the tribute.

Being far from the boss, the actual royal patron in Spain, the tribute became a problem causing selfish abuse. The encomendero usually acted like a tyrant, demanding service and serving punishment if natives don't follow. They demanded friendships and tribute, but declared war against the native if they couldn't give. Tribute was characterized as "excessive" and it was reported that encomenderos maintained stocks.[20]

The encomendero was charged with ensuring the well-being of the Filipinos—a duty to teach them a good Christian education. Unfortunately, the encomenderos did the opposite, treating the natives like delinquent military units than a community of human beings, abusing them by exacting both tribute and labor, causing the natives in later years to trust the friars over them. Encomenderos kept a quarter of the tributes, gave a quarter to friars, and sent the rest to the colonial government. Encomenderos maintained peace and order and helped the missionary work. The encomienda system gave the encomenderos a pretext for seizing land from barangay inhabitants. The encomienda system was abolished in 1720, but eleven encomiendas existed in the middle of nineteenth century.[21]

Luis Francia's book recorded more about the abuse:

> In addition, the local was obliged to render a certain amount of personal service to the Spanish, whether to the encomendero, the gobernadorcillo ("little governor" essentially the town mayor), or the parish priest. Men between the ages of sixteen to sixty were expected to donate their labor, known as polos y servicios, for forty days each year to so-called community projects. These ranged from servant work and the supply of foodstuffs to shipbuilding and military service, which in turn could be anything from crewing on a warship to working in artillery units. The exaction of forced labor especially in the felling of trees and the building of ships that continually disrupted livelihoods (such working on one's land) would be a constant irritant to the subject populace and perpetual incitement to rebellion.[22]

If the encomiendas become vacant and fell into the jurisdiction of the Crown, it was looked after by an alcalde mayor who collected tribute and answered only to Manila. Various government officials would take over their functions. In many instances, these abuses caused friars to complain, but they grew to be very much part of the colonial establishment; these diminished as their own abusive behavior increased.[23] Worship of Mammon/wealth obviously ruined the colonial good intentions, defining the truth/actuality how the royal patronage was—and causing then the native resistance.

Friarocracy: friar's rule in the Philippines next to encomienda. Many became Christians and so the demand of religious duties increased, including spiritual and material administration by friars. Abused natives by encomenderos are inclined to seek protection from religious man against their abusers. As the colony developed, religious order and civil administration were debating who were truly sovereign in the archipelago—the Vatican or Madrid? Patronato Real stated it clearly. The increase of prestige and material wealth of the friars led to power struggles. Friars highlighted the abuse of encomenderos to claim superiority over them. The power of friars as civilian administrators—with all the economic and social privileges granted to them by the king—gradually resulted the lowering of the spiritual and moral standard. Priesthood (to them) became an easy way of getting materially rich.[24]

Friars were supposedly under the monastic Regular Order and were cut off from the world with religious vows. In the Philippines, worship of Mammon/wealth came to play. Abuses created a picture that revealed that the good intentions of colonizers could be totally separated from the original ideas. In actuality, the situation was not necessarily approved by the one overseeing the idea or concept. What happened in the land subject to royal patronage is defined by how the representatives implement them, and so, showed what kind of government they asserted. Now, friars committed abuse of power in the Philippines that attempts to stop them by the assigned bishops were not lacking, but for so long was a failure. To stop the abuse and corruption, the bishop implemented his Visitation. A major reason for the ensuing corruption of the friars was land. The concept of owning land was introduced by Spain to the island. The bishop had no direct control over them (as not belonging to secular priests) and the friars could own land. In time, the clergy replaced the encomenderos, whose arbitrary and exploitative practices they used to denounce.[25]

Pastoral Visitation involved investigation of the parochial situation—to check the status of the parish and verify any possible anomalous acts, but this act was unwelcomed and hated by the friars. There were many visitation attempts by bishops, but friars seemed unbothered and continued their abuse of power for wealth. The role of the monarch as Royal Patron added to the problem, using it to do whatever it takes to maintain the order of royal patronage. Now, assuming the direct headship of the Church, he gave power to friars to head the towns they were in. During this time, the friars were the full embodiment of colonial domination. He was de facto a colonial civil administrator and a defender of the sovereignty of the King of Spain. Simultaneously, he was de jure by operation of the Patronato Real. In most towns, he was the only salaried government official that was entrusted with purely civil functions.[26] Friars drew taxes, served as directors of school, supervised elections, presided over meetings, approved ordinances, and maintained public works, such roads and bridges. He was the judge and guardian of public morals.

Indeed, he was the promoter, defender, and protector of Spanish rule in the Philippines.[27]

Friarocracy (government by Friars) served as good instrument for the colonial government because of its influence over the subjects who resisted the monarchial rule. Here is one example of the religion trapped in the position serving the political kingdom (not of God, but using the name of God). Indeed the Roman Church in the Philippines, with the effect of the monarch's ecclesial role, served the purpose of colonial Spain. "Church and State put into the hands of the religious (Friar) a tempting power which bore within it the seeds of abuse and corruption."[28]

To avoid the bishop's pastoral visitations, the friars argued that they would answer only to their Order Superior, which was not the diocesan bishop. Their argument was taken, but the Romanist Church responded by adopting the new alternative to change the rectorship (or pastorship) held by friars to secular priests in which the diocesan bishop could claim direct headship over them.

Unlike the friars, *secular* priests are designed to serve as parish priests under his Diocesan bishop (not to monastic Order Superior). *Secularization* of all parishes was the perfect solution to the needs of the situation. This was about the transfer of ministries run by friars to the seculars. This created a positive problem for the Filipino people. As secularization must be implemented, the shortage of secular priests made it impossible to fully implement. Part of the solution was that Filipinos must be welcomed to the vocation of priesthood. Friars must go; seculars must fully cover the parochial needs.

Slowly the move opened the door for interested Filipinos to become priests. Note that this priestly vocation became the first means for Filipinos to achieve higher education. What was not anticipated, however, was that in their higher education can help their fellow Filipinos to see the meaning of what had happened in their past. True enough, secularization served as vehicle for the Filipino separatist movement, culminating in the separation of the church from Rome during the Philippine Revolution. Indeed, humanness in historical sense must be stronger than religious dogmatism and folly.

The first Filipino priest to become vocal to the Filipino cause was Father Pedro Pelaez. Unfortunately, he died in a typhoon. Father Jose Burgos became the next leading figure for the Filipino cause, responding to the reality of their time. There were some Filipino priests—contemporaries of Burgos—who were active for the same Filipino cause. A brother of Marcelo H. del Pilar advised Marcelo to continue the cause advocated by Burgos.

After years, this priestly position with Filipinos became a serious threat to the interest of the Spanish monarch. In response, the Spanish king issued decree after decree removing the Filipino seculars from their posts, giving friars the chance to be returned to their parochial positions. The Filipino priests were naturally out of jobs to serve fully as parish priests of the Church. They were demoted to being coadjutors (acolytes).

Since the early years, the kings of Spain had been acting in favor of the friars and the interest of Spanish colonial territory. Exercising his power as *royal patron*, he had the final say to the Roman Catholic Church in the Philippines by removing all the Filipino seculars from their priestly posts. He listened in favor to friars who "have been utilizing the infamous use of undervaluing the capacity and fitness of the Filipino clergy *so* as to make themselves perpetual curates in the Islands."[29] The friars also had their own personal, selfish interests; the Filipinos thought hard about the government, the Church, and Catholicism. The monarch's use of royal power of patronage was based on his imperial interest—no matter how it sustained the abuses and corruptions offensive to the will of God for the people.

How the Romanist Church Served the Colonial Lord

Records tell us of many incidents where Romanist priests were exercising the work as pacifiers to the native Filipinos that were actively supportive to the freedom efforts. A shortage in the financial budget made Spain want to release the Philippines from its colonial responsibility. But Romanist Friar initiated by begging for continuing the Spanish control and use of power against the Filipinos. The obvious question was what would happen to the Romanist Church if the oppressive controller left them alone.

In 1619, news reached the Philippines that Spanish King Philip III (son of Philip II) might withdrew his rule in the country because of the expenses. Upon hearing this, Fray Hernando Mortega (friar priest) from the Philippines journeyed to Spain. He kneeled before the monarch, imploring him not to abandon the Philippines. The king said, "I will not give up what my father had conquered and left me."[30] This action represents the Romanist Church (RC) in relation to colonial power. What the priest is kneeling for is about power to control without mercy against their subject. Indeed, there is gesture of *idolatry* for position and power. Like the Romanist Archbishop Placido Louis Chappelle of New Orleans (USA), during his time, he persuaded the Americans to buy the Philippines from Spain with the amount of twenty million dollars ($20,000,000) just to keep the Philippines away from Filipinos, and be controlled by Americans.[31]

Many instances showed that the RC served the colonial master by pacifying the rebelling Filipinos by offering sure favor from heaven if they would not resist and submitted to the colonial rule. Fr. Geronimo Martin pacified the first Filipino revolt against Spaniard in Luzon, Lakandula, and Sulayman in 1574. Fray Santo Tomas pleaded for peace to the group of revolutionary Irrayas in 1621. Fr. Cristobal Fernandez urged the followers of Ladia's revolt in 1643 not to take actions against the Spaniards. Fr. Andres de Salazar pacified the Maniago's revolt in 1661. Diego Silang headed the Filipino revolt in 1762, but Bishop Bernardo Ustariz—who proclaimed himself provincial head—excommunicated Silang. Ustariz engineered Silang's liquidation.[32] Agocillo said about one cause of the failure of Filipino revolts:

> Filipinos were conditioned to live and feel apart from each other for almost 333 years. There was no sense of national unity ... there was a wide communication gap between the Filipinos ... friars, deliberately refused to teach and promote their language among the Filipinos ... Behind this ... was the fear of the Spanish friars that a Filipino who knew the Castilian language became better educated and, therefore, a future subversive or a filibuster.[33]

The first Filipino national secret society of the KKK-Katipunan was discovered by the Spanish authority on August 19, 1896 because of one member of KKK-Teodoro Paterno revealed the secret society to Fr. Mariano Gil. As his service to the colonizer, Gil reported this to the colonial authority.[34]

The Treaty of Paris was another anti-Filipino move with the Vatican. It brought together the American and Spanish representatives. The United States bought the Philippines with $20 million from Spain—and then the Philippines were surrendered by Spain to Americans, not to the Filipinos.[35] Apolinario Mabini implied that this was foul work because this treaty was agreed upon at the time when the Spaniards were no longer administering the Philippines.[36] By this, the Roman Church positioned itself as more in the business of securing its stability rather than advocating for God's love and justice for victimized Filipinos.

Religious institutional stability may be served, but if this becomes against the cry of the oppressed people for justice and human dignity, absolutely nothing left to call it "good." In this case, Church represented by RC seems wasted, not as flow of water that sustains life which 'the gate of hell cannot stop it' from quenching the thirst for salvation. History revealed to us that the Church manned by friars or some kind of men with callous hearts could do things that do not represent God—especially when the focus is secular stability and wealth. Honest and responsible humans must be reminded that not all actions committed by the Church represent the "kind of God" whom the Church is pinning. There are times that the Church was not, but it failed to distinguish and declare the distinction. Instead, it enjoyed the naiveté of the subject if the Church was not the maker of the naiveté.

Responses with Anti-Friar Feelings

On February 17, 1872, three secular Filipino priest and martyrs— Fathers Jose Burgos, Gomez, and Zamora (Gom-Bur-Za)—were unjustly accused as agitators of the local revolution. On January 20, 1872, the Cavite Mutiny was magnified by friars and others as a revolt designed to overthrow the Spanish rules in order to implicate the patriotic priests and their sympathizers. The three priests were unjustly executed by the garrote vil. Along with this, some fifty-two priests were sentenced to life imprisonment—and some were deported to Marianas, including some lawyers and businessmen.[37]

This affirmed the actual feelings of the Spaniards toward Filipino priests as "political dynamite." This became the turning point of the Filipino nationalist movement. As the conditions worsened after that revolution, oppression and abuse continued. The result of the killing of "their hope" priests—and the deportation of other intellectuals who could help oppose the colonial abuses—caused the Filipinos to realize that the situation was so serious that no normal person with heart and mind could not feel the pain.

As the result, in 1872, Filipinos launched the peaceful campaign for reformation, founded the well-known Propaganda Movement that would influence the Filipinos for their objectives. The Propaganda Movement was created to promote reform, equality, Filipinization, individual liberties. Graciano Lopez Jaena was a highly intelligent and was educated at the Seminary in Iloilo. When he saw the sad realities of the Filipinos, he started writing against the ignorance, abuses, and immorality of the Roman Catholic friars. This forced him to flee to Spain and he continued his work there. In Madrid, in 1883, Jaena founded the newsletter called *La Solidaridad* that published essays and articles about the Philippines and the Filipino situation. He died on January 20, 1896.[38]

Marcelo H. del Pilar finished his law course at the University of Santo Tomas (Philippines), and campaigned against the abuses of Spaniards. In 1882, he founded the nationalistic newspaper *Diariong Tagalog,* and wrote patriotic writings exposing the sad state of the country. Fr. Toribio del Pilar, his brother (one of the deportees to Marianas by Spaniard), said, "It is his obligation to continue the cause of Fr. Jose Burgos and them." In 1888, del Pilar wrote pamphlet after pamphlet ridiculing friar sovereignty and exposing the injustices committed almost daily against the Filipinos. He fled to Spain after intolerance. In December 1889, he took over the editorship of the *La Solidaridad* founded by Graciano Lopez Jaena. Marcelo died on July 4, 1896. In *La Solidaridad*, del Pilar in "Monastic Supremacy in the Philippines" stated:

> The Filipinos cannot look without sorrow at the powerful interference of monastic interest which impedes every fraternal current between Spain and the Philippines ... the friars impose on the government their dominance and they impose it with the pretext of warding off the treachery of the Filipino people ... We don't pretend to be unaware that Catholicism, reigning over the minds of the Filipinos, has to be the firmest and strongest bulwark of Spain in those seas ... The Philippines, under the religious dominion of

the friars, is not the Spanish colony that our forefathers conceived.[39]

Once a student at the University of Santo Tomas, Dr. Jose Rizal left the Philippines for Spain to pursue his study in 1882. He studied medicine, and enjoyed reading many books. He wrote his *Noli Me Tangere,* containing facts that he gathered while in the Philippines.

I have described the social condition ... I have unmasked hypocrisy which, under the guise of religion ... I have distinguished the true religion from the false ... The facts I narrate are all true and actually happened; I can prove them.

As said, the effect of the book on the Spaniards was tremendous. "All their defects, their ignorance, their immorality, their bogus culture, and their vices were faithfully mirrored in the novel." Trinidad Pardo de Tavera said, "All the defects of the public administration of affairs, the ignorance of the functionaries and their corruption, the vices of the clergy ... were made manifest. The prestige which the friars had enjoyed ... and the immorality and viciousness of the friars were exposed to the public view."

The book was attacked by Fr. Rodriguez. In 1889, Rizal published his answer and he exposed the ignorance of the friars. In spite of the forces that tried to prevent him, he worked harder for the welfare of the native land. In 1891, he finished his second book. *El Filibusterismo* was dedicated to the three martyr priests, Jose Burgoz, Mariano Gomes, and Zamora. He called them "victims of the evil."

Rizal understood the importance of their priestly roles for the Filipino cause. In Santo Tomas, he was able to convince his fencing partner, a bright law student (Gregorio Aglipay, later head of Iglesia Filipina Idependiente) to change his course from law to take up priesthood. He predicted that the Filipino people would someday need his leadership and service. From Madrid, Rizal returned to Manila and founded the *Liga Filipina*. Because of this initiative, he was arrested on July 6, 1892; on July 14, he was shipped to Dapitan, Mindanao, and lived there for four years. The Rizal's arrest caused Andres Bonifacio to found the secret society of KKK-Katipunan. Rizal was able to write his anti-friar feelings before his death. He wrote to Blumentrett, "I wished to hit the friars … I was forced to attack their false and superstitious religion, to fight the enemy that hid behind it."[40] He was executed on December 30, 1896, but won deathless glory as the "greatest genius ever produced by the Malay race" and as national hero.

Isabelo de los Reyes Sr.—a contributor to the *La Solidaridad*, noted patriot, and scholar—later cofounder of the Iglesia Filipina. He wrote about the abuses of friars in *La Sensacional Memoria*.

> Besides these shocking abuses, friars may even usurped land which the Filipinos inherited from their fathers simply by including it in their maps … That the friars ruthlessly persecuted those who dared to take their complaints to law … and ruining the many families thereby … That the friar bishops make one-sided change of curacies in favor of their brothers and prejudicial to the interest of the native priests … That the friars scandalously mock the laws and directives of

Church and state, bypassing them all with impunity …
That though they are supposed to be examples of Christian
conduct for their parishioners in the towns they administer,
they are the very cornerstone of scandal with their vices and
lasciviousness and their sacrificing the tranquility of decent
families to satisfy their carnal appetites.[41]

Church of royal patronage represented in Friarocracy of friars
who centered their interest on worship of Mammon truly became
the authors of social chaos and sustainers of discomfort and hatred,
making injustice to appear "divinely sanctioned." It is not God the
lord of justice that is represented by the Church then. Normal human
minds outside the bondage of doctrinism and religious claims can
see the difference.

The Sporadic Resistance for Freedom

The Creator of human nature designed us humans to react to what
is unjust to him. Filipino began to fight for freedom the moment
the Spaniards settled permanently in 1565 and continued until early
in the twentieth century. Lapulapu is among of those who refused
to bow under the Spanish yoke that cost Ferdinand Magellan's life
on 1521 in the island of Mactan.[42] History showed the Revolt of
Lakan Dula and Sulayman took place in 1574; they both lost their
kingdoms. The revolt stopped after they received a promise that
they would be treated well and their land and privileges would be
respected. The next Spanish governor broke that promise. Spaniards
oppressed the natives and seized their lands. The Tondo Conspiracy
of 1587–8 was organized by Agustin de Legazpi (nephew of Lakan

Dula) with the primary purpose of regaining freedom from Spanish rule. Many joined them like Magat Salamat (son of Lakan Dula), and many prominent native chiefs from Pandacan, Polo, Tondo, Navotas, Taguig, Candaba, and more. They even made an agreement with the Japanese and Borneans to furnish them with arms and warriors. When this was discovered, Agustin, Magat, and others were executed.[43] Part of human nature is to trust what is promised, but by deception, the selfishness succeeded. The spirit of freedom is able to unite people even from outside the boundary of race.

Records showed sporadic revolts from 1596 by different native leaders to 1744 of Fracisco Dagohy. Dagohoy's long revolt took place from 1744 to 1829; he was successful because of the desire of Boholanons to free their land from the bondage of Spain. The Agrarian Uprising took place in 1745 and 1746. Filipino tenants rose in arms and fought for what they considered to be their racial patrimony—ownership of Philippine lands. Diego Silang's Rebellion took place in 1762, proclaimed the independence of his people, and made Vigan the capital of free Ilocos. When he died, his wife Gabriela pursued his libertarian work. In 1762, the Polaris Revolt took place in Pangasinan. He established an independent government with Binalatongan as the capital.[44]

The sporadic religious revolts: The Revolt of the Igorots took place in 1601 when the expedition chaplain boldly entered the camp to persuade them to submit to RC Christianity and Spanish rule. This angered them and they killed the priest. The Spanish captain crushed them in a bloody fight. The Tamblot Revolt in 1621, a native babaylan (pagan priest) incited the Filipinos of Bohol to return to their ancestral religion and told them that the gods would help them against the Spaniards. They burned churches and attacked the garrison. In 1622, Bankaw was the chief who had welcomed Spanish Legaspi expedition at Limasawa Island. In his old age, he discarded Christianity and returned to pagan ways. Limasawa and Leyte rose against Spain. He and others perished in a battle. Hermano Puli's revolt took place in 1840–1. Apolinario de la Cruz, known as Hermano Puli, in 1815 was denied to become a priest because he was a native. He studied the Bible and listened to sermons. In 1840, he founded the Confradia de San Jose, which was banned by the Church and civil authorities. Against it, he continued his religious activities and won many followers from Tayabas, Laguna, and Manila. He was captured and executed in 1841.[45]

Gregorio Zaide concluded that all of these revolts proved that "the Filipinos even then had their racial ideal of freedom and that in the name of liberty they were ready and willing to fight and die."

The Cry of Independence and Freedom by KKK-Katipunan

The Kataastaasan, Kagalanggalangan, Katipunan ng anak ng Bayan (KKK), was a revolutionary movement founded by Andres Bonifacio and his friends. On July 7, 1892, in their secret meeting, after long discussion regarding Dr. Jose Rizal's exile to Dapitan (Mindanao, Philippines), they founded the secret society. The aim was to unite and obtain Philippine independence from Spain. The KKK minutes stated, "All should join this association, in which the reward is the freedom of the Motherland."

In the dark cave, Katipunero Aurelio Tolentino (a patriot and writer and later prominent member of IFI) wrote, "Viva La

Independencia Filipina!" This became the first recorded cry of independence. Emilio Jacinto, the "Brain of Katipunan" authored the teachings of the KKK movement.

> Life which is not consecrated to a lofty and just purpose is like a tree which casts no shadow—a poisonous weed. All men are equal, be the color of their skin black or white. One may be superior to another in wisdom, looks, or wealth, but they are equal as men.

The secret KKK was discovered by the Spanish authority in 1896 when one of the members confessed to Romanist priest Fr. Mariano Gil and revealed it to the Spanish authority. The Filipino first national uprising for independence then began. After the discovery of KKK, on August 26, 1896 Bonifacio tore his *cedula* (certificate of residency given by Spanish rule in the Philippines) and said, "Let us fight for our people's freedom!" Tearing that certificate signified the end of submission to Spanish rule.

The first battle of the revolution took place in San Juan del Monte on August 30, 1896. With nearly a thousand armed men, Bonifacio attacked the garrison; a bloody battle raged at the place now called Pinaglabanan. Spanish reinforcements rushed from Manila. Because of their inferior combat tool called *bolo* or *itak* (or large knife used as military weapons) Bonifacio and the surviving men fled, leaving 153 dead comrades behind. The flame of the revolution spread like fire. The towns in Manila rose in arms. In Cavite, Emilio Aguinaldo led the uprising. He fought and defeated the Spanish commander of the Guardia Civil in a single combat. This enhanced his prestige.

He struck in other towns, winning more victories. The Cavite revolutionists came to regard him as their leader.

Many Filipino patriots or revolutionaries experienced the terror of Spanish reign. Patriots were arrested and imprisoned at Fort Santiago, where they were tortured and executed. On September 4, 1896, four Katipunan were executed at Luneta. On September 12, thirteen martyrs were executed in Cavite City. On January 4, 1897, twelve patriots from Bicolandia were executed; some from this group died in prison or in exile. On March 1897, nineteen patriots in Kalibo, Aklan executed. About a thousand patriots were able to escape from the firing squad.

Fr. Gregorio Aglipay also became one active supporter of the Katipunan, founding a branch of the KKK called "LIWANAG" (Light) during his parish work as coadjutor priest in Victoria, Tarlac, on 1897. The Sanguniang Balangay (People's Council) voted Aglipay as Pangulo (leader). "The number joining increased daily and the town was converted to Katipunan with truly extraordinary speed ... But due to the signing of the Pact of Biak na Bato ... the activity ... was stopped."[46] Zaide said, "The Filipinos were determined to fight and die for their independence and the threat ... of execution could not stop them."

Many history teachers of Filipino students did emphasize much on foreign or Spain's good intentions—especially because the institution was the result of imperialist interests. They call them good guys in the field of events. But the said intention is just part of the whole picture. The Filipino revolutions were not against those foreign good intentions, but were a response to the facts of actual action that took place: abuse, injustices, prejudices, racism, deceptions, sins, selfishness, and worship of wealth that became the reality. It revealed how far the invaders could regard the Filipinos as unequally human as they were at the time. The man-made darkness in the actual scene was not the good intention or a reflection of the mightiness of the living, loving, liberating Lord. It was blindness as they believed "man is not created equal." They felt higher than others and favored by God. The Filipino revolutionaries knew the reality of their inferior weapons, but the greatness of godly and moral reasons were overpowering. They pursued the struggle—even to the point of death.

Seeing Freedom as a Gift from God

Revolutionary leaders like Andres Bonifacio laid down rules of discipline to be followed by the KKK members.

> Love God with all your heart … Bear always in mind that the love of God is also the love of Country, and this too, is love of one's fellow men … Punish any scoundrel and traitor and praise all good work. Believe, likewise, that the aims of the KKK are God-given for the will of the people is also the will of God.[47]

We don't know where the invaders got the notion of "inequality of humans." Seemingly these revolutionary people were more human in the way they understood life by this time. In some of Bonifacio's work, we read, "Rely in God and don't be taken in by our enemy who has the ways of an animal … Ah, give us your love, Heaven that looks upon us, God, my Lord, don't deny to your children the protection they ask for."[48] He was confident that the desires of revolutionary hearts were not offensive to the purpose of God, but to change the evil realities that time shaped by "the ways of an animal."

Emilio Jacinto is like American Thomas Jefferson in the Philippines. He acted as the "the brain of revolutionary Katipunan," authored its rules, and talked about the equality of all men.

> God is the father of humanity, and what the father requires of his children is not constant protestations of respect, fear and love for him, but the performance of his mandates, which are the mandates of reason, hence the true respect and obedience to the dictates of reason, and to them we must adjust all our acts, words, and movement, because reason originates with God himself ...[49]

We know that, in the spirit of struggle, Jacinto gave reason to the revolution to fight for the created notion of human inequality. The slavers were offensive to God's purpose and must be broken. Respect and love must be restored; by nature or human design, all must find the way to sustain and celebrate it.

Apolinario Mabini was the "brain of first Philippine government." Facing the war against Americans, we read his thoughts with godly tone.

> But no matter. Let us fight to our last breath in order to defend our sovereignty, our independence. If the North American nation is great and powerful, greater and more powerful still

is Providence who watched over the unfortunate and who punishes and humbles the haughty.[50]

He got the message of Jesus in beatitude when Jesus stood as "teacher/preacher" and gave hope to the poor of the kingdom of Roman Caesar. Mabini also wrote a Decalogue.

Thou shalt love thy country after God and honor more than thyself; for she the only Paradise which God has given thee in this life, the only patrimony of thy race, the only inheritance of thine ancestors, and the only hope of thy posterity. Because of her thou hast life, love, and interests, happiness, honor and God ... Thou shalt strive for the independence of thy country for only thou canst have any real interest in her advancement and exaltation; and her exaltation thine own glory and immortality.[51]

Mabini believed that God loved all people, provided all things for all humanity, and that the nation is the sanctuary of one particular people or race that must be preserved and must be free to grow into its full potential and not be hindered by the one who empowered the notion of inequality.

Emilio Aguinaldo may have had wishful thoughts about the United States as the revolution continued in the American era.

And earnestly entreat them to proceed to the formal recognition of our struggle for Philippine Independence; certainly they are the forces designated by Divine Providence to maintain equilibrium among the people by sustaining the cause of those who are weak.[52]

The spirit of how the United States of America became a nation should be stated and not forgotten as a reason for its relationship to the Philippines. Filipinos must remind them—as anti-imperialists did—that freedom should be the reason and not a bait to go against it.

Generally, the Filipino revolutionaries believed that God was in their side too, because God gave everyone the ability to see His truths and absolute good for life. Those that acted the opposite must be using lies and deceptions to be successful against others. With that, such actions must point the sacred design of human feeling and the designer of human's ability to stand what is right.

Freedom as the Reason for Struggle

There is a need to point out the very issue of human history into clarity; it was not for the sake of killing the "giant" or to prove something like revolutionary bravery, that in spite of their inferior weapons, they stood fought for freedom against superpower.

In 1896, the Philippine National Revolution for Freedom and Independence took place. Writings in these years were instruments of telling and introducing the revolution. Andres Bonifacio wrote, "Bear in mind that the cause of our sacrifices is the realization of the dreamed liberty of our native land that will give us freedom and will vindicate the honor that, through slavery, was interred in the grave of incomparable oppression."[53]

Bonifacio dreamed about liberty of the land as home of the beauty of Filipino humanity, as opposed to oppressor's slavery of which the full nature to be human in their land is suppressed. God gave the ability and faculties to grasp the wisdom of who their Creator was. True as it was, the oppressor is to be seen as maker of "human anger," creator of human's discontent in the environment with bullying machine of the "winner," trapped to keep the notion of life as "competition" in the darkness of inequality —as opposed to "for God so loved the world" (John 3:16).

Bonifacio said, "In order that the sacredness and honor of our country be made complete, in order that the whole world might witness the nobility of our character, let us not emulate our enemy in this detestable conduct of the war, let us not go to battle merely in the interest of killing, but rather in defense of the liberty of our country, and thus fighting cry out at the top of our voices: Mabuhay! Long live the sovereign people of the Philippines!"[54]

He saw the reaction to the injustice done to sovereign people as an opportunity for the world to see and understand. It is in defense against the enemy that is already inside their homeland—for freedom—not naïve enough to see themselves as good only to be oppressed. Human as they were, they can understand the meaning of freedom, like a mission to be fulfilled announcing that Filipino knew what is "worth dying for." To feel for freedom and sanctity of life is itself a reflection of the designer of man's heart. History is a vehicle for actual events to be mirrored and truth displayed.

In "Light and Darkness," Emilio Jacinto said:

Liberty is the attribute of man from the moment he is born; thanks to it, he thinks and does as he pleases, provided he does no harm to another. Liberty comes from Heaven and no power on earth is entitled to appropriate it, nor have we a right to consent its being done ... There are instances when Liberty is smothered by error, by the blind worship of ancient bad practices and laws suggested by crafty henchmen. If there is right, it is because there is liberty; liberty is the column that sustains the edifice and the audacious one who tears it down in order to bring down the building must be annihilated.[55]

Freedom sometimes is used to do harm or violence against those who wronged us, but basically freedom is not to smother or to suppress or to destroy our own freedom, but to celebrate our humanness with it—the nature of our being. If not suppressed and pushed to do the opposite of it by human nature, our joy, security, and complete exercise of our being can be done only with other humans. Knowing that we cannot live alone and "no man is an island," only those who pretended to be in the jungle of the beast cannot see the sacredness of freedom. From birth, the seed to value freedom is already planted. It is part of every human being (everybody knows that); one is willing to be alone or die alone for it. It is a built-in moral sense. Liberty comes from heaven—so in man, we see God. With my Christian persuasion, I should say "God put it there," except that others denied it for themselves.

In writing "Liberty, Equality, and Fraternity," Emilio Aguinaldo said, "People of the Philippines, the hour has come to shed our blood to conquer our right liberty. Let us band ourselves about the flag of the revolution, whose motto is Liberty, Equality, and Fraternity."[56]

Romanist Catholic's friars were the first target to eliminate by revolutionaries as the community's "very cornerstone of scandal," dragging and indentifying God to their selfish immoralities. The Filipino intellectuals understood the evils, abuses, violations, and immoralities (political and social) done to them, but the ordinary masses also felt the actuality and truth of it. Here, religious title or name is identified as not necessarily the same with the spirit of Christianity or the very purpose of God in the function of the Church that blesses life. Filipino revolutionaries may have hated the system and men in the Romanist religious structures or institutions, but not the Christianity of Christ.

III
The Struggle for Freedom in the American Era

Some revealing actions and reactions will lead us to see in human nature and the capacity to build the community for human life in which we can make sense of our Christian faith. Here, it is just right to think the meaning of the crucial event in life: What is the root cause and how people react? What sort of things does the event bring? Revelation of the design is seen in human actions. How can God's purpose in us stand as an answer to the man-made darkness? We need to see the man-made darkness can cause the "Light of the world" to be needed—or is God needed to be pushed out of this world? Is the purpose of God in life served, or is He truly irrelevant? Did God make serving the policy and agenda of the market-driven? Are you blessed if you have the capacity to consume material products?

History cannot selectively avoid tackling idolatry and false prophecy in man—like in olden days (Jeremiah 23:25; Roman 16:17; Galatians 1:6) for *niceness* or nicety. To be critical is one honest attitude responding to what is made powerful and enthroned and the name of God is used. Making sense of Christianity is the way of making sense to live with purpose. Humans deserve to find a way of life that is eternal and sustainable. What is not should be identified. If God is not, then what is the "greater power" to defeat the rival (others) must be is? But the thinking is one from the culture of "survival of the fittest" seeing life as a contest, in which appeared ridiculous the teaching of Jesus saying "whoever wants to become great among you must be the servant, and whoever wants to be first must be your slave" (Mtt. 20:26), is Jesus wrong about this?

Aglipay in Spanish Leaders, Revolutionary Government, and the Filipinization of the Church

A community must be built according to the truth of man and the truth of the Designer in which everyone must aim to base the order of life. Gregorio Aglipay was led to that position in history. The scene was provided by the actuality of war. The war with Spain and America caused Americans from Hong Kong led by George Dewey to go to the Philippines.

Part of the turning point in history was done its first action in the Philippines. To make us understand how this new era came to be, we must understand how the Spain and American started the war. On April 20, 1898, the United States Congress passed the resolution recognizing the independence of Cuba from Spanish rule, which it says authorizing the use of armed forces to drive out the Spaniards. As the result of this, on April 24, 1898, Spain declared war against the USA, but the first action of this war was done in the Philippines. Weeks earlier, in the absence of the Secretary, the

Assistant Secretary of the Navy Theodore Roosevelt secretly alerted Dewey to move against the Spanish forces based in the Philippines. As Dewey complying and preparing for war, he established secrete contacts with Emilio Aguinaldo as Filipino recognized nationalist leader. "On April 30 evening Dewey entered Manila Bay, at daybreak he opened fire on the Spanish fleet at 5,000 yards ... when smoke had cleared all ten of Admiral Motojo's ships had been destroyed. Dewey after this, he asked for more troops from America to take and hold Manila.[57]

The war was not fully over as some Spanish forces still in the land. Known to the Spanish Governor General Basilio Augusto and Roman Catholic Archbishop Bernardino Nozalida that Fr. Gregorio Aglipay is the most influential Filipino priest during this time, they gave him task to perform, hoping to gain the Filipino support to fight against Americans.

The two Spanish leaders together commissioned Fr. Aglipay to convince the Filipino revolutionary leaders: Mariano Trias, Artemio Ricarte and others to bring them back to Spanish side now that the Americans is in the colony, and that they should continue fighting against the Americans. But Filipino faith in the promises of Spain was already gone. This time, Emilio Aguinaldo looked at the Americans as a Filipino ally against Spain. So, upon his arrival from Hong Kong, knowing about the necessity of talking to Aglipay, he sent an emissary persuading Fr. Aglipay to work for the Filipino cause.

Archbishop Nozalida countered this move by commissioning Fr. Aglipay to convince Aguinaldo of the Spanish cause. But Aguinaldo was firmed this time to cooperate with the Americans over Spaniards. So, he urged Aglipay to go north part of the region to work for the Filipino revolutionary cause. Nozalida encouraged Aglipay to ignore and not to heed for Aguinaldo but instead, go and investigate the condition of the diocese. Here, by the goodness of Aglipay in religious duty, he did what Nozalida asked of him, he secured the release of two political prisoner Jesuit priests, then, he proceeded to Cavity and joined Aguinaldo's revolutionary movement.[58]

June 12, 1898, was the Declaration of Philippine Independence, the formal organization of the Philippine Revolutionary government. Apolinario Mabini, chief adviser of Philippine first president Aguinaldo, and president of the cabinet, served notice that the Philippine government was no longer recognizing the authority of the Roman Catholic Archbishop Bernardino Nozalida, "the Revolutionary government … refused to recognize the authority of the archbishop. It prohibited Filipino priests from accepting any position from the Catholic Church without first securing the approval of the Revolutionary government"[59]

In October 1898, President Aguinaldo issued a decree appointing Fr. Aglipay as Philippine Military Vicar General, which made him the religious leader of the new Filipino Revolutionary government. As Catholic priest, he owed allegiance to the Church. But as Filipino he owed allegiance to the Revolutionary government. Faced by this dilemma, Aglipay chose to be "Filipino first and Catholic second."

Doing his job as a religious highest chaplain, Aglipay issued a letter to all Filipino clergy urging them to organize themselves into a cohesive body geared to the national emergency. This is part of building order in all sectors of the new government. Aglipay urged the creation of a council that would petition the Roman Catholic pope to appoint the Filipinos in all Church positions from archbishop to the lowest parish priest. The idea was going toward complete Filipinization of the Catholic Church—this idea was originated by the Philippine government and Mabini. Aglipay also urged the Filipino priests to unite in the interest of the country because the Philippine government "cannot recognize as head of the Filipino clergy any Spanish bishop." The hypocritical Church of the friars was finished as headed by the Spaniard. The Church of Christ must continue to stand to do its ministry free from justifying the injustices committed in the past. The Church must be free from pinning the name of God in the worship of wealth, position, and prestige. The Church must not protect the agenda of pro-Spaniard and pro-friars—not the kind of Church that had no capacity to see the heart of man/victim, ignoring the life/people over its hiding place of dogma and aiming to please the powerful imperialist of security. The Church must be free from the panicking Spaniard; instead, it must serve the people of the nation ruined by the injustice and racism of the time. It must have the capacity to see the message of the Kingdom of God as liberating, and about love, justice, righteousness, and brotherhood.

In November 1898, Aglipay obtained his official appointment as Ecclesiastical Governor of Northern Luzon from a political prisoner, Roman Catholic Bishop Hevia Campomanes. Campomanes did a favor for Aglipay by ordaining eight Filipino priests and deacons presented by Aglipay. Along these chances, Aglipay was endorsed by his co-priests for the position because of the "very great good which has done for the Catholic Religion … during the recent insurrection."[60] Aglipay was given a full administrative power—

almost like a bishop—that enabled him to mobilize the Filipino clergy for the Filipino cause.

The Filipino delegations in Rome asked for Filipinization, but the pope was more inclined to listen to the friars and consequently promised nothing to the Filipinos. That same day, these delegates announced their withdrawal from the Roman Church in the Spanish press.[61] This civilized approach for Filipinization of the Catholic Church in the Philippines was not successful, but revealed the callosity in the part of the Romanists. We know that many factors can make a religious institution numb (no matter how much religious name is put in it) against the cry for justice and respect for the crying soul—even if this was coming from the brown race. The process to complete the Filipinization of the Catholic Church was stopped due to the Philippine-American War that eventually led the end of Philippine government.

The 1898 Treaty of Paris between Spain and America

The battle in Manila Bay between America and Spain was followed by Aguinaldo's creation of the new Revolutionary government outside Manila, but the American and Spanish command planned the mock Sham Battle in Manila (walled city).

In August 1898, the Spanish command in Manila and US officers representing Admiral Dewey conferred behind the back of Aguinaldo and the Filipino nationalists in their position outside Manila. An agreement was reached that after the sham battle, the Spanish would surrender to the

US military on the condition that the Philippine nationalist should be excluded from Manila. To this condition US officials readily agreed. As planned, the mock battle took place, Spain surrendered and the US military took over Manila from the Spanish, which later, came into direct confrontation with the Filipinos."[62]

The Peace Commission dated October to December of 1898, was created to discuss the final peace terms between Spain and the United States in Paris. Later the treaty was called the Treaty of Paris. In this move, the newly proclaimed Filipino government sent Felipe Agoncillo (lawyer and patriot) to participate in the peace discussion, to help the case of the new Filipino government. There, he was not permitted to attend this conference because the Filipino government he represented was not recognized by the two groups (Spain and America). In the creation of the treaty, as said above, the Romanist Church played its role as "brought together the American and Spanish representatives … in order to overpower the Filipinos." Spain was forced to turn over the Philippines to the Americans, who agreed to pay $20,000,000.

The Treaty of Paris was signed on December 10, 1898. Understandably, the Romanist Catholics panicked because the Philippine government was indirectly taking over the ecclesial authority. The treaty did not go into effect until the US Senate ratified it.

In USA, during the heated debate about whether or not the Philippines should be taken, President William McKinley had an audience with a group of visiting pastors or ministers. 'After he prayed, it came to him to take them (Filipinos) all to educate, uplift, civilize, and Christianize them, and by God's grace do the very best we could by them, as our fellow men for whom Christ also died."[63] On the other hand, enough senators believed that the treaty was *unfair* to the Filipinos and must be rejected. But the imperialistic desires of the US Republican leadership at that time were strong enough. On February 4, 1899, the unfortunate rupture of Filipino-American hostilities happened and many who were opposed to ratification changed their decision to vote for it affirmatively.[64]

False news took the role! The American propaganda made it appear that war had started, and the Filipinos had "fired the first shot." President McKinley said that the fighting has begun when the "insurgents" (Filipinos) *attacked* the American forces. Senators who were against the ratification now voted for it. Who fired the first shot is an important moral issue. Those who felt that the Filipinos were victims of unfair treatment maintained their opposition to imperialism. The truth was known later. "American soldiers testified that the United States had fired the first shot."[65] No matter how the served lies came to be known, the truth didn't change the course of Filipino-American war.

On February 6, 1899, the treaty was ratified. The wealthy textile manufacturer W. B. Plunkett invited McKinley to speak in celebration of the ratification of the treaty. It was the biggest banquet in the nation's history. In Boston, McKinley said, "No imperial designs lurk in the American mind." That same night, Postmaster General Charles Smith said, "What we want is a market for our surplus."[66]

McKinley's Market for Surplus as His Economic Solution

It is important to understand the past in order to understand how and why the following subject took place. One of the questions that Americans and Filipinos were asking was how the United States became imperialist when the reason for its being a nation was to protect and promote freedom. Mabini "insisted that America should recognize their independence, but instead, waged war on them." The anti-imperialist George Hoar believed that America's "war of glory was converted into a war of shame." To understand, it is the contention of the following subject.

During 1893–1897, many of the most powerful American industries began to believe that their survival depended upon the markets of the world. William McKinley said that the *economic depression* must have a solution. LaFeber tells that changes of the situation had initiated when President William McKinley entered his office in March 1897. He assumed presidential power with the promise of restoring prosperity. His first inaugural address revealed his intention as "to cooperate in friendly fashion with the businessman."[67] He was able to make the Congress believe it and support it. He stressed his beliefs in his appearances before the National Association of Manufacturers (NAM). In its first convention in 1895, McKinley showed his perfect program: "Our own markets for our manufacturers and agricultural products and a reciprocity which will give us foreign markets for our surplus products."[68]

In June 1897, McKinley sustained his pro-business stand in a joint meeting of Philadelphia Museums and the Manufacturers Club.

"There is no use in making a product if you cannot find somebody to take them (or consume or to buy them). The maker must find a taker. You will not employ labor to make a product unless you can find a buyer for that product after you made it."[69] McKinley believed that he had found the key to the doors of foreign markets. Seven months after entering the White House, McKinley told the Commercial Club of Cincinnati, "No subject can better engage our attention than the promotion of trade and commerce at home and abroad. Domestic conditions are sure to be improved by larger exchanges with the nations of the world."[70] After nearly a year as president, McKinley warned the NAM that the depression had not yet fully lifted because "of their present insufficient facilities for reaching desirable markets."[71] The president's ability was fully appreciated by close associates and observers. Theodore Roosevelt, after discussing foreign and naval policies with the president, remarked with wonder, "He shows an astonishing grasp of the situation."[72]

We can see in this subject that McKinley and the Americans during this time were looking primarily to themselves, to be saved from the depression as we know in the argument of the opponents of the imperialism in the next subject below. The economic drive really divided the country and changed the course of American history.

The Push for Market-Driven Imperialism with Religious Sanction

After the Spanish-American War, President McKinley said, "What to do with Spain's former colonies, primarily the Philippines?" Expansionist groups that included business people, called for American imperialism. In this desire for territory and opportunity for market, they claimed that it was America's "destiny" to be a great world power. Bring back the memory of the Manifest Destiny before the Mexican war.[73] Manifest Destiny was a term used to describe the belief in the 1840s in the territorial expansion. Those who believed in this maintained that because of American economic and political superiority, and its rapidly growing population, should rule all of North America. The phrase was first used in 1845 by John L. O'Sullivan in an article regarding annexation of Texas. The spirit of Manifest Destiny was revived at the end of the 1800s, during and after the Spanish-American War.[74] Many business leaders supported the idea of expansionism because it would open up new markets for their product and also a golden opportunity to access to natural resources of other nations and to bring new raw materials into the country.[75]

The idea of "market for surplus product" as General Postmaster Charles Smith mentioned during the celebration of the ratification of the Treaty of Paris (on February 6, 1899), had already been heard in U.S. Congress since 1884 from men who justified the request of naval construction in commercial and expansionist terms. Senator John F. Miller of California declared, "The time has come when manufacturers are springing up all over the land, when new markets are necessary to be found in order to keep our factory running."

Finally, in 1890, Captain T. Alfred Mahan published *The Influence of Sea Power upon History*. It argued that only a large Navy could protect the trade that would be the lifeblood of the new American empire.[76] It has been the desire in which in actualization, this "lifeblood" was viewed as the killer of American ideals. To others, it was a killer of culture and valued racial identity of other nations.

The new empire propagandized the world with sweet justifications for the new empire to "civilize and Christianize." This caused big questions among the American politicians because the Philippines is already a Christian and civilized nation in many ways. Historians wrote that "the Spanish converted most Filipinos to Catholicism and established schools and a centralized government. Manila's oldest university was older than Harvard. By 1898, much of the upper class, the illustrados, had been educated in Europe. Aguinaldo convened a national assembly comprised of doctors, lawyers, professors, and writers."[77] We know that even in the language of Filipino revolutionists or reformists against Romanist's friars and Spanish monarch royal patronage that they demonstrated their Christian convictions, in their writings and teachings, encouragements, poems, in pursuing the call to independence and for respect to their human dignity toward the creation of new nation.

The American Protestant as believer of imperialism, served (like a deceiving instrument) as powerful justifications for empire. But the truth in history revealed that it is not primarily for Christianization and civilization, but territory and market. As we can see in the concept adored dearly by the foremost among the "jingoes," Theodore Roosevelt "vigorously preached" the expansionist doctrines of the eminent naval historian and philosopher of imperialism, Captain Mahan. This is the primary reason which is adored and served by Roosevelt from Mahan, he said "Affirming America's destiny to look outward beyond national borders ... argued that the nation's honor and prestige as well as her defense and trade, depended upon the acquisition of numerous overseas naval bases, the control of the Caribbean and trade routes to the Far East." Mahan said, "Beyond the broad seas, there are the markets of the world that can be entered and controlled only by vigorous contest ... To affirm the importance of distant markets, and the relation to them of our own immense powers of production, implies logically the recognition of the link that joins the products and the markets—that is, the carrying trade."[78] In 1897, Theodore Roosevelt delivered a speech on preparedness to put Mahan's concept into action, then met widespread approval throughout the country. After McKinley's murder, Roosevelt served his imperialistic desire fully when he became the twenty-sixth president from 1901 to 1909.

Protestant missionaries "provided a spiritual rationale that complemented Mahan's idea of navalism; sought to convert heathen unbelievers in faraway lands ... Many came to believe that the (Filipino) natives first had to become Western in culture before becoming Christian in belief.[79] Of course, this was viewed by the opponents as "good intentions in a wrong place to exercise" because of the fact that Philippines is already Christianized and civilized. If this was because of the empowered lies saying that Roman Catholic in the Philippines is not to be considered Christian for the sake of imperialist justification, it shows that those kinds of people are capable of playing ignorant if "drunk with the desire for power and wealth" able to claim whatever that serves the idolatry of power in which God is to be the means for that ends. Honest and good intentions based on invented notions of racial superiority played here too. "They eagerly took up what they call 'the white man's burden' of introducing supposedly civilization to the 'colored' races of the world. But they opposed direct military or political intervention."[80]

Anglo-Saxon Doctrine is what many Protestants at the time became preachers for. It was a doctrine and racial theory that the *white race* that had evolved in part out of Social Darwinism. Lodge, Roosevelt, and others expansionists were influenced by this theory. Whereas Herbert Spencer had applied his doctrine of "survival of the fittest" to relationship within society, followers such as Harvard historian John Fiske and Congregationalist minister (preacher or pastor) Josiah Strong applied it to relationships among different races and cultures. In separate publications of 1885, Fiske and Strong wrote that the Anglo-Saxons (British and Americans) were (people) obviously more fit to govern than were other peoples. According to Strong's book *Our Country*, the Anglo-Saxons were "divinely commissioned" to spread their superior political institutions throughout the world. Based on that claim, it is said that it was not a betrayal of American ideals to take over other lands. There was a racial and religious duty to do so. Strong believed that races eventually would die out.[81] Historians revealed "among the elite was a cult of Anglo-Saxon superiority with the concept of a breed endowed by nature to rule, an idea of obvious usefulness to white Americans ... religiously inclined exponents of racial superiority believed it had a divine sanction."[82] Strong said that Anglo-Saxons were "divinely commissioned to be, in a peculiar sense, his brother's keeper." Of more importance than this book in turning America toward expansionist sentiment were Protestant missions established abroad. The Protestant missionaries were the first converts to the new definition of the American mission."[83]

Social Darwinism had a big influence in US expansionist imperialism. The phrase "survival of the fittest" was coined by

Herbert Spencer. From scholars, academics, and scientists came racial theories and justification of expansion. Charles Darwin's *On the Origin of Species* (1859) had popularized the notion that among animal species, the fittest survived through a process of natural selection. Spencer argued that the same laws of survival governed the social order. When applied aggressively to justify their desire, Social Darwinism was used to justify theories of white supremacy as well as the slaughter and enslavement of nonwhite native populations that resisted conquest. When combined with the somewhat more humane through "white man's burden" of Christian missionaries, conquests included uplifting natives by spreading Western ideas, religion, and government."[84]

Laissez-faire issues in the Gilded Age are where the irony in American Protestantism began. The term is from French for "leave it alone," used by President Andrew Jackson who had view that government as much as possible should leave the society and economy alone so that natural social and economic forces could operate freely.[85] In this issue, like businessman, Protestant ministers gave support to laissez-faire and about status quo they provided religious sanction for the businessman's view on property, inequality, stewardship, state aid, and labor.[86] Mark Hopkins, congregational minister/pastor and president of Williams College said, "Love requires the acquisition of property because it is a powerful means of benefiting others." Those who have done the most for our (American) institutions have been men with "a strong desire of property ... as men now are, it is far better that they should be employed in accumulating property honestly ... than that there should be encouraged any sentimentalism about the worthlessness of property."[87]

Since the businessman was the dominant figure on the American scene during the years from 1865 to 1901, Andrew Carnegie's thoughts about acquiring wealth received strong support (those Protestants who like his idea went beyond). In the Gilded Age, nowhere, however, did the business spirit find greater favor than in the Protestant Church. Urban Protestantism cultivated the middle and upper classes that possessed the ultimate power in American society. Never before had wealth mattered so much to the church. Wealthy business figures were appointed to church boards in increasing numbers and men of business were in demand to serve as church officials. Even the Baptists, who prided themselves on being a poor man's denomination, ceased to express contempt for wealth and decided that the man of wealth was also "a man of talent." The churches were fast becoming "social and religious clubs for privileged classes."[88]

Inequality of human beings is consistent with Darwinism, as businessman do, the churchman accepted inequalities among men as inevitable and desirable and maintained that those who had risen to the top were the men of ability whereas those who had failed had only themselves to blame. Henry Ward Beecher (pastor of Plymouth Congregational Church) said, "God has intended the great to be great, and the little to be little." As in "general thought," he said, "No man in this land suffers from poverty unless it be more than his fault unless it be his sin." Bishop of Massachusetts said that wealth comes to the man of morality. To desire wealth is a sign of strong character and is both "natural and necessary."[89] Carnegie's *Gospel of Wealth* accorded with Protestant's ideas of stewardship. Lawrence said, "If ever Christ's words have been obeyed to the letter, they are obeyed today by those who are living out His precepts of the stewardship of wealth." President Joseph Cummings of Wesleyan University said, "The great remedy for social wrongs" was to "be found in the Christian use of wealth." The majority of Protestants took a negative view of social reform and state action, for they considered reform a matter of individual regeneration rather than of improved social conditions.[90] Baptist Russell Conwell, author of *Acres of Diamonds,* preached the "gospel of success." He said, "I say that you ought to get rich, and it is your duty to get rich." The richest people are generally those of the best character. It is wrong to be poor.[91]

Roswell D. Hitchcock of the Union Theological Seminary stated, "Capital represents intelligence, self-denial, and control and is finer than labor, just as brain is finer than muscle. At bottom, is an immorality to fight against the inequality of condition, which simply corresponds with inequality of endowment."[92] Threatening, offensive, and strong enough that there was a movement in the pages of *Communist Manifesto* that read "for an end to laissez-faire capitalism on the ground that it did not let anything, not even human life, stand in the way of profit.[93]

Clergy who resented on the "aristocratic drift of Protestantism" denounced the alliance between church and market. Reverend Arthur T. Pierson said "The communion of saintliness is displaced by the communion of respectability. Our churches are becoming the quarters of a monopoly."[94] Market-driven with religious enthusiasts is absolutely making the bad notion against the Church in their justifications of expansionism. But Heffner was right that "this is America's Gilded Age, an age of aggressiveness ... when concern for the traditional principles of public and private morality had been supplanted by the worship of Mammon (Wealth, richness and possession)."[95]

The Filipino-American War and the Objections by Anti-Imperialists

Before the ratification of the 1898 Treaty of Paris, McKinley had already issued the proclamation indicating to assume control of the Philippines, followed by the sending of the US troops. "Economic motives certainly played a significant role in the decision to fight for the control of the Philippines, which were located closed to the hotly contested and potentially lucrative China market."[96] To implement actions by a powerful leader who detached his human heart from his subject (Filipino/colored/ "inferior") for the sake of a capitalist agenda of which he is serving, now must learn numbness and callosity in heart in playing and applying his power to satisfy the pro-market agenda with lies. Mark Twain said, "They (Filipinos) look doubtful, but they are not. There have been lies; yes, but they were told in good cause. We have been treacherous; but that was only in order that real good might come out of apparent evil."[97]

Filipinos were outraged by the treaty, so that even though they had fought "alongside American troops to defeat the Spanish now began fighting the … American troops." Aguinaldo then ordered his troops to fight "war without quarter to the false Americans who have deceived us!"[98]

The advancing American empire, one author said, "Managing an empire turned out to be more devilish than acquiring one"[99] Three years of Filipino war for freedom and independence against this new invading empire of America happened. America "used $600 million to defeat Filipino Pres. Emilio Aguinaldo." Before it was over in 1902, some 126,500 American troops served in this war; 4,234 died, 2,800 more wounded. Filipino casualties were much worse. In addition to the 18,000 killed in combat, an estimated 200,000 Filipinos died of famine and disease as American soldiers burned villages and destroyed crops and livestock.[100]

Jack Estrin said "Many anti-imperialist voices cried out; among them were the voices of Cleveland, Bryan, Schurz, Mark Twain, William Dean, Howells, and William James. They insisted that conquest of the Philippines would make a mockery of democracy and establish America as a nation of immoral hypocrites."[101] As we learned from St. Augustine, I would say that the devilish reality of this war cannot escape from the heart of (God's designed in) man, felt and entering into "the depth of the soul, and with the eye of the soul saw the Light that never changes casting its rays over man."[102]

The Anti-Imperialist League in the United States was created and founded in September 1898, vigorously opposed both this unjust war and annexation. They included "some of the nation's wealthiest and most powerful figures."[103] "Ex-presidents Harrison and Cleveland were part of this league. The major anti-imperialist arguments pointed out how imperialism in general and annexation in particular contradicted American ideals."[104] Mark Twain who made his reputation as a humorist, could find nothing funny in the Philippine adventure. He stated, "We have crushed a deceived and confiding people; we have turned against the weak and the friendless who trusted us; we have stamped out a just and intelligent and well-ordered republic; we have stabbed an ally in the back and slapped the face of a guest ... we have debouched America's honor and blackened her face before the world. We should change our flag." Twain suggested one "with the white stripes painted black and the stars replaced by the skull and crossbones."[105]

In a bitter satire, Twain assured Americans that the "Blessings-of-Civilization Trust had the purest morals, high principles, and justice cannot do an unright thing, an unfair thing, an ungenerous thing, an unclean thing."[106] Andrew Carnegie wrote a letter, dripping with sarcasm, congratulating President McKinley for "civilizing the Filipinos … About 8,000 of them have been completely civilize and sent to heaven. I hope you like it."[107]

The Anti-Imperialist League "carried on a long campaign to educate the American public about the horrors of the Philippine War and the evils of imperialism … Whatever their differences on other matters, they would all agree with William James" angry statement: "God damn the US for its vile conduct in the Philippine Isles."[108] From Cleveland to Speaker Thomas Reed, from Sam Gompers to Andrew Carnegie, they implored the Republic to resist the temptation. William J. Bryan declared, "The fruits of imperialism be they bitter or sweet. This is one tree of which citizens of a republic may not partake. It is the voice of the serpent, not the voice of God that bids us eat." [109] Bryan attacked the Republicans by saying that "they had departed from the ideals of the Fathers of America and were following in the footsteps of old Rome by conquering and ruling subject races."[110] Worthy to our Christian pondering, Bryan said to his Republican opponents, "They would have known that hatred of an alien government is a natural thing and a thing to be expected everywhere. Lincoln said that it was God himself who placed in every human heart the love of liberty …"[111] It is brave for him to say such words in which Filipinos must be affirmed.

Historians cannot ignore the fact that these were observed by thinking human beings; wrong or evil conducts are identified in spite of the powerful flow for the opposite: "Mostly Democrats and former Populists resisted the country's foray into empire, judging it unwise, immoral, and unconstitutional."[112] The brutality of the war troubled some Republicans too. George Hoar, a Massachusetts senator and founder of the Republican Party, fought the annexation on moral ground. He said that America changed the Monroe Doctrine, which is about eternal righteousness and justice.

A doctrine of brutal selfishness looking only to our own advantage. We crushed the only republic in Asia. We made war on the only Christian people in the East. We converted a war of glory to a war of shame. We vulgarize the American flag. We introduced perfidy into the practice of war. We inflicted torture on unarmed men to extort confession. We put children to death. We devastated provinces. We baffled the aspirations of a people for liberty.[113]

Other objections were that the Asian people could not be assimilated into our tradition—and that imperialism would lead to militarism and racist dogma at home.[114] If the anti-imperialists in North America could recognize injustice as they condemned them, in the Philippines, Filipinos are not naïve at all, and so fought against it. Filipino Apolinario Mabini in 1899 wrote that it is the Treaty of Paris that the Americans and Spaniards agreed together at a time when the Spaniards were "no longer administering the Philippines, thanks to the victory of our arms ... from the very beginning I have insisted on the recognition of our independence, but the American government has consistently refused to promise to recognize our independence and instead, waged war on us. The Americans promised to help us secure our independence and you saw that they fought us because we refused to abandon our independence and allow ourselves to be ruled by them." [115]

Richard Heffner said, "But it was also America's Gilded Age, an age of aggressiveness, of unbridled acquisitiveness, of coarseness and vulgarity, when concern for the traditional principles of public and private morality had been supplanted by the worship of Mammon. By 1900 American businessmen had guided the nation to such heights of material success that she entered the new century a stridently powerful industrial giant."[116] What Heffner said was the reason of invasion of the Philippines. "Worship of Mammon or wealth" captured spirit market-driven imperialism. Materialist success meant destruction of the helpless defender of Filipino nation's freedom. Invader imperialists were "not mad" and no justification of invasion but did it anyway just because they could. This tells us what kind of culture was developed in the spirit of inequality which is absolutely offensive worship against the holy, just, loving, and merciful God of life.

American Christian missionaries, acting as an ally, justified the Republican agenda to the philosophy and policy of capitalist's imperialism—truly it gave Christianity a bad name. Again, Bibliolatry (heresy in worshipping the Bible) and "dogmatism" is another game played like more than the moral issue of life. As one

Romanist Church's belief said, "Voice of the people is the voice of God." Exercise persuades people to one "majority-Church" so that the voice of God is theirs, and the blood of the victims is counted for nothing and not worthy of Christian reflections. No, Christ's revolutionary teaching is to live love from self to others—even people of color and even to the enemy and unlovable. It is sad to say, but worshippers of power and wealth are more interested in things than pleasing the God for life/people.

Some of the attitudes and actions that led to this new role are described as "jingoistic." In the 1850s, a British song about a war was popular. "We don't want to fight, but, by jingo if we do. We've got the ships, we've got the men, we've got the money too!" From this song came the word "jingoism," which means, too much nationalism. As America's world role changed during the late 1800s, some people said that Americans were becoming "jingoistic."[117]

Filipino Priests for Total Separation from Rome

On the eve of the Filipino-American war, Fr. Aglipay acted as the religious head under the Philippine Revolutionary government, he ordered offering prayers in the time of war, Blessed Sacrament to be exposed, and priests to dress as captains in the armed forces. While Aglipay was Military Vicar General, he wore the uniform of a lieutenant general of the Revolutionary Army. In the second year of this war, President Emilio Aguinaldo was captured in 1901 by the Americans in way of treachery. In that year and the next, many leaders surrendered to the US forces, including Aglipay. The last

Filipino leader who continued the war was General Miguel Malvar; his surrender in 1902 marked the end of Filipino-American War.

On May 8, 1902, during the time of his birthday, Fr. Aglipay called the Kullabing Assembly, attended by Filipino Catholic priests his wartime comrades. In that gathering, they had long discussions on Church situations. One of the priests suggested their total separation from Roman Church. Aglipay concluded, "It would be better for them to separate from the Holy Father (Pope) completely. The religion that they would then establish would be the fruit of the recent revolution watered with so much Filipino blood."[118]

Aglipay's concept of Church was definitely not chained by doctrine/dogma-isms or claims that potentially blinded the eyes of the oppressed and the oppressors, but instead, it was about the truth of God revealed in the teachings of Jesus Christ. It must be understood by man in his deepest reflection of the reality of human being in situation—in his deepest agony shaped by the forces of selfish man-made darkness—and felt by the innermost feeling of the human devastated by injustices in history to the highest state of complete hope in God (as in IFI Epistle) to "go alone fixing the spirit and mind to God." This Church should be understood as the product of man's reaction and responding to the reality of injustices, disrespect of racial identity, and to no capacity to see man equally. This Church should witness God's truth to the world revealed in human nature and designs, demonstrated, revealed, and tested in history. This Church should not limit its understanding of the truth of God by literal reading of the Bible. This Church that sees God not only that we analyze the existence of God according to the manifestation of the creation, but to see that human feeling (heart), mind (thinking), and human strength are not dead or discounted in understanding the greatness and nature of God manifested in a normal state, honestly obeying the order of his humanness should his fullest nature standing on the ground of what and where and when reality occur. Truly and honestly complete, free humans must demonstrate the "image of God" that in history this "living being" human must engage. This Church is not imprisoned in the pages of the Bible and can be manipulated by men who worship wealth, Mammon, prestige, and position. This Church should teach and witness God that in Him is life. This Church should liberate the pro-people teachings of Jesus, and have the capacity to recognize in man what is offensive to the pro-people/life message of God. This Church is not a product of doctrinal formulation unbothered by the darkness of the unjust, abuse, corruptions, and devilish unjust and ruinous illegal war. It is the bearer of truths that are witnessed by learned humans after his real and most painful experiences in history as the result of ultimate evil darkness, now witnessing the Light of God as the answer to all these man-made conditions and the "absence of Godly love."

On July 4, 1902, Roosevelt proclaimed that the Filipino-American War was ended. This did not mean that aspiration for freedom and independence was also ended. IFI/PIC historian, Father Apolonio Ranche stated, "In the whole archipelago, from the countryside to the cities, many Filipinos, been on resisting American colonial master. In the field of journalism, nationalist writers, such as Aurelio Tolentino, Juan Matapang Cruz, Juan Abad, and many others were active in Manila and nearby provinces coming out with symbolic literature. (Vicente Sotto of Cebu did the same thing). Meanwhile, various groups continued the armed struggle. Macario Sakay and his lieutenants proclaimed a Tagalog Republic. Fausto Guillermo, Luciano San Miguel, and others continued armed resistance near Manila. Up north, Roman Manalan led resistance in Pangasinan and Zambales. Valentin Butardo raised the banner of resistance in Ilocos Norte. In Isabela, Manuel Tonines was at the forefront. Even the so-called Messianic groups joined the cacophony of resistance: the Guardia de Honor in Pangasisnan and Ilocos, the Santa Iglesia under the leadership of Felipe Salvador in Central Luzon, and the Colorum with Ruperto Rios at Babaylanes under Papa Isio in Panay and Negros."[119]

Filipino expression of their desired liberty was varied and sporadic in the American era (as happened in Spanish era). These expressions for liberty made us see how the American regime in the Philippines offended or threatened by it. Laws and acts against those who still expressing their desires against imperialism must be implemented. Laws and acts were reflecting the evidence of the truth of these Filipino movements. In 1901, the Philippine Commission (sole legislative body) passed the Sedition Law that forbade the Filipino advocacy for independence even by peaceful means. The Brigandage Act (1902) classified all Filipino armed resistance as pure banditry. The Reconcentration Act (1903) gave legal justification for a hamlet to deny the Filipino guerilla fighters the support from the local populace. The Flag Law (1907) prohibited the display of the Philippine flag and the playing of the Philippine National anthem (March National).

In this period of continuing resistance, when the institutional and American missionary Churches were cooperating with the

American imperialism, the nationwide Filipino Church, nationalist Catholic in nature, (the IFI) was established. In spite of these laws, the Filipino-IFI Church served as a vehicle of their sentiments for justice, respect for humans, freedom, and independence. They taught liberating Christian *truths* would bring national freedom. They wore the prohibited Philippine flag to be displayed, as a vestment in celebration for Christ salvific act during their liturgical worship or Eucharist, which has been the center of Christian worship since the beginning of Christianity. During the lifting up of the highest salvation of all humans embodied by the body and blood of Jesus Christ, the Filipino played "March National" (now the national anthem). While the elevation of the Blessed Sacrament at the Eucharist, they sang the theme for God and for country as the highest expression in their deepest agony against anti-life. We elevated the Christ of God—the Christ of man's salvation, and the Christ of life and hope of all. They affirmed and celebrated it, vested with the highest nationalist sentiments.

IV
A Church Shaped with Historical Sense

IFI: The Congregation of New Men Proclaimed by De Los Reyes Sr.

Isabelo de los Reyes Sr.—one of the Filipino intellect and scholars—was in Spain to the persecuted intellectuals of his time to continue their advocacy about respecting the Filipino people as human beings. In Spain where Lopez Jaena, del Pilar, and Jose Rizal continued their works to awaken the world in comfortable darkness regarding Philippine situations. Scholar and writer Isabelo de los Reyes translated his New Testament Bible, when he learned that "only the Romanist Church in the Philippines is wrong not the entire Christian Religion." There, in his newspaper *Filipina Ante Europa* he called, "Enough of Rome! Let us now form without vacillation our own congregation, a Filipino Church, conserving all that is good in the Roman Church and eliminating all the deceptions which the diabolical astuteness of the cunning Romanists had introduced to corrupt the moral purity and sacredness of the doctrines of Christ."[120]

By this time of Philippine turmoil, the slogan was already heard: "An Independent Church in an independent Philippines." Returning to the Philippines early in 1901, Isabelo campaigned for the establishment of the new Filipino Church. On July 1901, Isabelo organized the first labor union in the Philippines, and 1902 formally established the Union Obrera Democratica (UOD). The founding of the labor union gave broad basis to the new nationalist religious movement that would serve as a vehicle for the pro-life/pro-people messages of the Church—liberating and pro-love for the people or humans who were affected by the darkness of political and religious imperialism and were using the Bible or religion to justify their selfish, racist, pro-material, and capitalist expansionism with religious doctrinism propelled by Anglo-Saxon and Social Darwinist enthusiasts.

Understanding the environment of the founding of IFI, this nationalistic Church would be a Church that offered some preservation of the spirit of Christianity that seemed to be gone by the religion of laissez-faire capitalism, and in the ways of religious Romanist of popularity contest. Following that action, the concept of the new Church—Christianity—should be rescued from deceptions and lies justifying things for the success of imperialist isms, or from the playful user of the name of God as a crown permit to conquer and as "blesser" of the survival of the fittest philosophy. In that context, the nationalistic Church should offer some alternative to the Church of "Jingoism" (expansionist over nationalism) that was hurting the sovereignty of Filipino people. The American Church allied with the imperialist idea, the product of their love for their own race, and for the chances of "wealth" in the agenda of the powerful giant nation. They say 'detach from the world, don't worry about your political situation, your nation, and your worldly problem; think about the spirit and heaven only, that you have place in heaven when you die.'

By that time, the IFI should be proclaimed as a vehicle of the oppressed people of the "inferior nation." The Philippines must have a Church product of their heart, mind and soul (their totality) reminding them that Christianity and Church of God is about love for all people inclusive and embracive even to the brown Filipinos. Their struggle for equality and fairness of all people is counted and should not be hidden for reflection of the salvation of God. Church should not be forced to be a servant of the cult of racism that appeared to be instrument to what is hurting the poor and the humble, who needs more of the Savior?

On August 3, 1902, at the Union Obrera Democratica meeting at the Centro de Bellas Artes, Manila, Isabelo de los Reyes Sr. proposed the establishment of the Filipino Church independent of Rome, with Aglipay as the Supreme Bishop. The proposal was embraced and loudly proclaimed by the people. This Church was to be called the Iglesia Filipina Independiente (IFI) or Philippine Independent Church (PIC).

To give dignity to the new Church movement, Isabelo placed people for the executive committee, including Howard Taft and others. Among those names, only Emilio Aguinaldo was ready for the position as the honorary president. Aglipay at first did not welcome the move and for total separation. But the masses who understood the meaning of the new Church composed the first adherents. The people's movement, including Protestants, sixty

Navotas, and numerous Tondo residents, members of the UOD, Filipino clergymen coming from the Roman Church, seminarians, Vicente Sotto and his Intelligentsia movement of Cebu were followed by municipalities, millenarian groups, etc; Toward the end of the year, fourteen Filipino priests, affiliated to the new church, followed by the defection of Fr. Pedro Brilliantes of Ilocos Norte. Agoncillo stated, "There was no stopping now, and priests from all over the country came rushing in to sign their names in the roster of Filipino Church." In October 1902, Aglipay accepted the position to which he was elected as Supreme Bishop.[121]

IFI as the People's Initiative

One may ask who really founded the IFI or PIC. Isabelo de los Reyes Sr. once said that he did and some historians agreed. Apolinario Mabini once said that without him pushing Fr. Aglipay to organize the Filipino priests for Filipinization during the Revolutionary government, "there is no Philippine Independent Church today." Of course, some correctly pictured it as the people's movement. Let us consider the incorrect picture by some.

Some Romanist authors aimed to reduce the importance of the PIC and discredit some personalities of the founders. One popular incorrect view is that Aglipay founded his own Church to become a bishop and to have a wife. We still hear this with other intimidations in provinces by CFDs (Catholic Faith Defender). Those are some examples of dishonesty or lies that somehow reveal the nature of the Romanists believing the usefulness and effectiveness of lies (helped by the ignorance of the subject). Some say, that the IFI was founded by Aglipay—a native church to an affiliate of the Episcopal fold"

[S. Mayuga]. Another said, "Aglipay was the first Filipino cleric to break away from the Catholic Church when he found his Protestant sect in 1902."[122] "It is known popularly as the Aglipayan Church after its founder Gregorio Aglipay … in 1965 … joined the Old Catholic Union of Utrecht." [Achutegui and Bernad]. The Catholic Encyclopedia stated that Aglipay schism "organized in 1902 by a priest of the native clergy as the Independent Philippine National Church with himself as archbishop.[123] If you read further, you can see lies in these statements. The description is almost unrecognizable to the IFI members; it seems to tell us of a totally different Church. It serves their purpose because they wrote them that way, but clarity, honesty, and truth of engaging human suffered. Picture of honest humanness that can show the greatness of God—the maker of our being human who has the capacity to resist what is devilish—is suppressed by man's selfish intents. This shows that serving the institution is almost the opposite of serving the God of justice and truth that designed humans who has the capacity to recognize and respond to what is unjust.

Though Filipino people loved this name "Aglipayan," associating it with General Padre Gregorio Aglipay, the Romanist "educator" who gave name Aglipayan has different purpose. Allied with American imperialists, they consistently called the IFI "Aglipay" or "Aglipayan" for the derogatory purposes of putting it down. The message that wanted to be the conclusion is that IFI is Gregorio Aglipay's church, his own initiative for his own ambition. IFI can witness that this kind of way is really a working tool by others with ungodly motives. Not of God? Absolutely! Trapped by concerns for stability, control, and numbers (to satisfy the phrase "the voice of the people is the voice of God"), some Romanist authors consistently used phrases that brought unclear picture to come out with the wrong conclusion. It seems that believing the power of lies, but it results as judgment in the end.

The IFI movement became a target of myth making and lies. One honest University of Santo Tomas (UST) historian Pedro Gagelonia said, "The founding of the PIC, to the mind of the ordinary student of history, is surrounded with mystery. This partly due to the fact that majority of our historians choose to relegate almost to obscurity the role played by the PIC in our nation building."[124] This should not be because, as Gagelonia said, by all means every historian is duty bound to preserve the "sanctity of true historical facts." The truth is that the Filipino people of different stories within two ranges of the imperialist era are the one who founded this religious movement. The different stories means clergy stories, resident stories, Katipuneros, intellects, individuals, women, labor, peasants, congregations, etc.

Now, let me be honest to my intention of writing this book again. Let me try to attempt to lay some bedrock of theological reflection. I understand that the greatness of God is not limited according to the perception of imperialist man or oppressed man. (In the creation theology recorded in Genesis (2:7), God breathed in man when He created them to be "living being," and what is "living being" is not to say "flesh only" neither "spirit only," neither brown race or white or red, or yellow, and black person only, but "living being" is from element from earth and the breath and spirit of God). Our subject is not to struggle for theological justification to claim for anything (for theology as we accepted it is already in the Bible), but we have no reason to continue speaking things if the giant racist and prejudice mind in our judgmental exclusivist "abnormalities" is not broken. I believe it is pleasing to God to free ourselves from what hinders each of us from embracing the ability to enliven the love of God for all people in the world that Jesus subjected. He said, "To go and make disciples of all nations … and teaching to obey everything I have commanded you." This must be said not to ruin all nation, to make exploited subject to selfish mammon worship.

Thus, the Filipino race is counted as part of the image of God—shaped and breathed—so how they behave responding to their world situation must be counted part of the definition of the living being. That being said, to *discount* them in obeying their human nature designed by God to feel disgusted of the injustices cannot be reconciled with the very purpose of God, is simply not right and offensive to God. Apolinario Mabini said, "If the North American nation is great and powerful, greater and more powerful still is Providence who watched over the unfortunate." We should not disregard this understanding. God uses the affected, the bullied, called "indio, negro, backward" (seems just to justify the guilty conscience of the offenders). But God uses those whom justice is denied for His justice. Beliefs gave Filipinos strength and confidence.

This corrects the myth and confusing lies that the IFI/PIC was founded because of one's ambition. Take for example the Intelligentsia group in Visayan, Cebu, led by Don Vicente Sotto, when Isabelo de los Reyes Sr. published the new proclaimed PIC, the group in Cebu published it through *Ang Suga* (Light) of Sotto, and they requested a PIC priest after that. The result of Ang Suga in Cebuano speaking Mindanao caused people in Mindanao to organize themselves too as "Filipinista" (Filipinist-PIC/IFI). A group of women in the Pandacan

Church—in a patriotic act—dragged the friar out of the Church and closed the church door from the Romanist priest. They opened the church later for Fr. Aglipay as the new PIC head. Fr. Vicente Ramirez of Lagonoy, Bicolandia, affiliated the PIC with the whole municipality and the church building. Many more local histories are like these.

As a fact, Gregorio Aglipay preached those places to become members of IFI, but with their various experiences and stories, in their human response helped them see the message of God's love and justice to be celebrated in the nationalist Church. Local experiences of the people preceded the event making them ask Aglipay to lead them. One IFI Bishop Remollino said, "The IFI was founded by one and a half million Filipinos in which Bp. Gregorio Aglipay was not more than one." Aglipay said, "The Filipino people are my witnesses that I am not the author of the Filipino Church … The PIC was founded by the people of our country. It was a product of their initiative, a product of their desire for liberty, religiously, politically, and socially"[125]

In February 1903, KKK Aurelio Tolentino said, "You all recall the history of the Revolution. You have seen the road through we passed, and know it is an irrigation ditch filled with blood. We manage to reach the goal of our ideals, but it all vanished like a dream …. But no … our political independence may be dead, but from its ashes our religious independence arisen vigorously …"[126] In a Philippine social science study, one concluded that PIC is neither the offshoot of any singular condition nor the work of any one man. It is rather "a result of collaboration between compatible and conflicting circumstances and personalities."[127]

Felipe Buencamino (once recognized as one of the three pillars of the IFI with Aglipay and de los Reyes) wrote to Aglipay. He said, "I have been helping … of emancipating the PIC from the slavery of Rome because I consider the enterprise very beneficial to our beloved people for the fallowing reason. The Roman religion does not represent the love of God because there is no love where there is no liberty and where there are superior and inferior races. What results from these differences is domination and slavery, the former is for the superior race and the latter for the inferior." [128]

IFI's Initial Teachings and Liberating Belief

The Filipino cause in revolution was not about killing just because they can, and not about how brave they were, even though they really were, but it is about being human with principles and historical sense. It was not about against personality—not anti *who,* but above all *for* freedom, respect, justice, honor, national dignity. Although they cannot avoid that to fight for principles, they target people, but people are targeted because of the philosophy behind the principles and actions. They knew what life is all about; therefore they knew what it is that they were willing to die for.

Basically Filipinos were friendly people. As history has proved, their trusting and friendly ancestors welcomed the Spaniards: Raja Kolambu and Siago made blood compact with Magellan; Bankaw of Limasawa, Sikatuna, Sigala of Bohol welcomed Legaspi. They fought for freedom from injustices, abuses, grief, and sin. Through individual, group, intellectuals, masses; in religious and secular reactions, they addressed religion, government, and economics.

Now IFI Church is a vehicle of those coming from unsuccessful venues for freedom. It saw God as the end of all evils done to Filipinos. IFI held and proclaimed freedom as God's purpose. As God called Israelites to be free after four hundred years of slavery, He demanded freedom. "I have heard the groaning of the Israelites, whom the Egyptian are enslaving … Therefore, say to the Israelites: 'I am the Lord, and I will bring you out from under the yoke of the Egyptians. I will free you from being slaves to them … I will take you as my people, and I will be your God'" (Ex. 6:5–7). Filipino freedom has been denied to them for four hundred years. If "freedom" is causing the Bible to be written, it should cause people to appreciate the Church of Christ. Filipinos knowledge about "freedom" can be traced back to Lapulapu. As in organized and unified means, our last fight for freedom was in 1902 when General Malvar surrendered. In the same year, the IFI was born.

The initial teaching of the IFI was seen in its Fundamental Epistles and in the Doctrine and Constitutional Rules. For this purpose, we put emphasis on freedom as perceived from the past. The IFI Epistle VI initially taught Liberty, as "its worth is understood only when is lost; it is only seen as lovely when man is in the prison cell." It warned that man should not wait to completely lose the opportunity to celebrate the equality of man of being complete not in the environment of "winner and loser." It continued to say that a free man "is a complete man, dignified, honorable, of lofty sentiments, attended by all his rights and by his unavoidable duties as well; but a man who becomes a slave of his own free will is a man with a vile heart, a deceitful, object sycophant—a person, in short, deserving of pity." The Epistle continued:

We are born with the right to think freely and express our thoughts according to the light of reason which the Divinity has given us; we are born with the right to associate freely with those we choose for the purpose of our own perfection and needs; we are born with the right to govern our own persons, our families, home, and birthplace; we are born in short, with the right to do freely whatever is our pleasure so long as we do not violate the liberty and rights of others. We Christians have been called to liberty (Gal. 5:13), since Jesus has come to free us (Luke 4:18; Isa. 61:1). Man has the obligation to defend these liberties of his for which God has given him heart and brawn, just as another animals and creatures defend theirs.

And he who does not know how to defend his liberty is the most despicable of beings and merits all the tyrannies, cruelties and most incredible outrages of the master to whom he faintheartedly submits. So God permits him to find his punishment in his own cowardice. Liberty is one of the most precious gifts with which the Creator has favored us; so it is that we may in no way the purest morality and right conscience impose on all things. "The perfect law is the law of liberty," according to the general Epistle of St. James (1:25). It is a principle which the Philippine Independent Church proclaims and all philosophical schools sanction that where there is no evil intent there exists neither a crime nor a sin; and that where there is no such ill will, man is free to do all that is not repugnant to his conscience."[129]

For the imperialist people of the island, the first tool is education and claims to keep the oppressed thinking "inferior." Therefore, it is not impossible for man of colonial mentality to stay inferior. Deception wins bondage to act superior in the part the oppressor, a trap that must be overcome. The oppressed and the oppressors must be free from the mentality we made that "humans are not equal." Man must be able to live sustainably with others equally, and so live sustainably happy and equally.

Notice that in that concept freedom didn't put up any boundaries in terms of time and race. In relation to this, Epistle III says, "We have valiantly shaken off the heavy religious slavery of four centuries of obscurantism." IFI is the "crowning glory" of libertarian struggle started even from Lapu-lapu. The spirit of what they fought for is in the thinking of IFI.

IFI's Catholicity is about God's love for all—not about control and place. "Our Church is Catholic because in reality, it is profoundly cosmopolitan by conviction and sentiment, considering all men without any distinction children of God, and it bears the designation 'Philippine Independent' only to identify it as an association of free men who, within the said universality, admit servility to no one."[130] As opposed to the oppressive concept, this Catholicity is not centering on the visible Romanist headship. The inclusive Catholicity centered on Christ emphasizing the *brotherhood* of all men for the *fatherhood* of God.

"Revolutions, therefore, are perfectly providential, and despite them causing us momentary disasters, they ultimately bring the far-reaching redemption and result in benefits that will bless many generations to come. They are like typhoons which, in the twinkling of an eye, destroy and erase secular vices and abuses."[131] (This is in response to those who tried to discredit the said Filipino revolution). Valuing freedom is a kind of worship to the One who planted it in everyone's heart.

The teaching places Psalms in the hands of the faithful. "Praise Jehovah, O my soul, he who made the heavens and the earth … he who gives justice to the oppressed; he who gives bread to the hungry; he who sets prisoners free; he who opens the eyes of the blinds; he who love the just …" (Psalms 146:3) [from IFI Epistle 111].

IFI says, "And he became human to redeem us and teach us to love all creatures not excluding our enemies, we call him Son, because such humanity proceeded from his Divinity …" [Epistle III; also in "Doctrine and Constitutional Rule of the PIC"]; Loving the enemy is Jesus' revolutionary concept for sustainable peace. "Let us leave the Romanist, then with their aggressions, and simply answer them with silence. We go our way with spirit fixed on God" [Epistle 11]. This suggests that we go our way (from being devastated, trampled upon) to be in the loving embrace of God; alone with the loving Father; in closely focus on Him. IFI intends for its members to have close relationship with the loving God.

"We repeat that we do not repay hatred with hatred, and would now wish to be like the sandalwood, which perfumes the very axe that destroys it …" [Epistle 11]. The IFI Church taught its members to be peace makers. Loving our enemy is real peace formula—a real Christian moral revolution. It is not right to challenge the Serpent with its same way, it only justifies its evil ways. The word of God is our sword against it. Though it is said 'Do not forget, beloved brethren, what our most beloved Jesus said about guarding false prophets who come to you in sheep's clothing but which are ravening wolves'" [IFI Epistle 11].

PIC as of God is the result of experience of the past—when Filipinos were called as "nothing," "indio," "backward," second-class people. PIC was people treated as "nothing," but out of nothing came something—a Church of God. PIC held its pillars: liberty, reason (science), love, and scripture. God demanded liberty for His people (Ex. 3:10). Jesus preached salvation from sin and work of Satan; it is about liberty (freedom) from evils and evildoers, wicked powerful violators of human liberty; Liberty of those with desire to live according to his/her racial nature/identity to enjoy being under God. The Bible said "Christ set us free that we might remain free men … Brothers, you have been called to be free men" (Gal. 5:1; 1:13; 4:26, 31; 1 Cor. 7:22; 2 Cor. 3:17).

IFI Epistle says, "Freedom is a gift from God." Love is the summary of God's law/commandments; it is the answer to all the cry of the oppressed and deprived, victims of injustice and selfish assertion of opportunity to rule. The Bible says, "Love is the fulfillment of the law" (Rom. 13:10). Jesus by example taught Christians to reason out their faith; He did it against Satan; religious leaders, and opponents. Jesus said, "I need to preach the Kingdom for this is the reason why I was sent" (Lk 4:43). The Bible says, "Come now, let us reason together" (Isa. 1:18). Jesus said, "For this very reason I came" (Jn 12:27). IFI had godly reasons to fight for freedom and believe in the lordship of God. It takes the right reasons to get out of deceptions that enslaved people. Satan used the Word to make Jesus think of "self" and submit to the temptation, but Jesus reasoned in preparing for salvation work lays ahead for people (rather than self). The Bible said "be wise" and "not naïve." As Christians, IFI believes the Scripture that everybody should practice what is in it that serves the purpose of God and fulfills His commandments. The Bible stated, "All Scripture is God-breathed and is useful for teaching, rebuking, correcting, and training in righteousness, so that the man of God may be thoroughly equipped for every good work."(2 Tim. 3:16). Scripture is our source to learn to do good and what to rebuke as evil. It is absolutely our guide for what is right and just. IFI held that the actual experience of the people is to make sense that the Bible is indeed God's breath for life.

IFI's Early Liturgy and Worship

The liturgy emphasized worship, prayers and novenarios (devotionals) of IFI phrases on freedom and independence. In its famous liturgical worship *Misa Balintawak* says, "Oh, God Almighty, embrace our native land, we fervently hope that the day will come when we will see the glorious day of our freedom, the day of our independence." (*O Bathalang Maykapal. Ampunin Mong aming bayan manatili nawa O Bathala, ang maligayang araw ng pagsasarili, ang maligayang araw ng pagsasarili.*) [132]

IFI's liturgy allows expressions of Filipino sentiment during the time of suppression: 1) Wearing the Filipino flag as vestments during the time when anti-flag law was implemented. 2) Words of encouragement to continue aspiring for freedom in a nonviolent way. 3) Singing of the nationalist song like in *Misa Balintawak*. In the elevation of the Sacrament, the "Marcha Nacional" is played. 4) IFI believed in God's guidance for her leaders. In the "Katapusan" (ending) of *Misa Balintawak*, it says, "May your guiding hand be upon our leaders for the good of our countrymen. Adopt the Filipino Church and grant the clergy with wisdom and goodness in guidance to the path of Your holy word and commandments." (*At bigyan Mo ng palad ang mga pinuno upang mapaginhawa, ang mga mamamayan. Ampunin Mong Simbahang Pilipino at pagkalooban Mo ang aming mga pari ng talino't bait sa pagtataguyod sa amin patungo sa landas ng mga banal Mong utos at aral.*)[133]

IFI's Ecumenical Relations

Keep in mind that the IFI/PIC, though independent, is not independent in advancing the purpose of God for all people. Epistle 1 discussed "seeking other Churches to consecrate IFI clergy." As situations demanded, after Aglipay's acceptance of the position as Supreme Bishop, his next step was to confer with Protestant brothers in and outside Manila so that they could work together for the purposes of God. Unfortunately, Protestants at that time were not friendly to the IFI. However, in 1948, a relationship began to take place when PIC Bishop Isabelo de los Reyes Jr.—father of the National Council of Churches in the Philippines (NCCP)—received the gift of Apostolic Succession from the three bishops of Episcopal Church of the USA.

In 1961, PIC established the formal concordat relationship with many Anglican Provinces. The Concordat of Full Communion between the PIC and Episcopal Church was signed 1961. The core of agreement stated that: (1) "Each Communion recognizes the Catholicity and independence of the other and maintains its own; (2) Each Communion agrees to admit members of the other Communion to participate in the Sacraments; (3) Full Communion does not require from either Communion the acceptance of all doctrinal opinion, sacramental devotion, or liturgical practice characteristic of the other, but implies that each believes the other to hold all the essentials of the Christian faith." [134]

Text of the agreement with other Churches stated almost the same as of Episcopal Church. From 1961–5, Concordat with other Anglican Provinces worldwide was established: Church of the Province of West Indies, Central Africa, West Africa, East Africa, Church of North India, Church of Ireland, Episcopal Church of Scotland, Lusitanian Church, Anglican Church of Canada, Anglican Church of Australia, Church of England, Nippon Sei Ko Kai-Japan, Church of Uganda, Rwanda, and Burundi; Spanish Episcopal Reformed Church; Church of the Province of South Africa; New Zealand; Church of Melanesia; and Episcopal Church of Brazil. Then in 1965 with Old Catholic Churches of Austria, Germany, Holland, Poland, Switzerland, Croatia, Czech Republic, Polish National Catholic Church of America. It was established with the autonomous Episcopal Church in the Philippines (1997); Church of Sweden (1995); and the United Church of Christ in the Philippines (UCCP). PIC is a full and participating member of the following ecumenical bodies: World Council of Churches (WCC), Christian Conference of Asia (CCA), and the National Council of Churches in the Philippines (NCCP), in which Bishop Isabelo de los Reyes Jr., son of the cofounder of the IFI, was the first chairman.[135]

The concordat or ecumenical fellowship among Churches continued. This proved that independent Churches around the world had no intention to be *alone* as literally independent, but with others, equally respecting the independence and Catholicity. They celebrate in equality and doing the mission of God to promote, preserve, and protect life as intended by God, to promote justice and peace and the integrity of God's creation.

IFI Concordat with ECUSA

IFI looked at the concordat (sisterhood) relationship with ECUSA (Episcopal Church of the USA) seriously and positively. The ECUSA had the same historical beginning as IFI/PIC. I cannot see any reason why it would not work together for the Kingdom based on the fact that the business of the Church should respond to the call of Christ who was sent by God to the world where and when Roman Empire affected the "people of God." Now come the situations, the same call that these churches should respond proclaiming the "love of God for all."

The first Episcopalians like George Washington, James Madison (who became Episcopal bishop 1790), Thomas Jefferson, and Patrick Henry were "all powerful advocates of civil liberty and profound believers in religious liberty."[136] Thomas Jefferson was called "the pen of the American Revolution" (while George Washington as the sword). He established his reputation when he wrote, "The God who gave us life, gave us liberty at the same time."[137] These Episcopalians were believers of the Declaration of Independence that inspired the Americans fighting for freedom. The most important was the belief that "all men are created equal."

Connecting that to the Philippine revolution, Emilio Jacinto— the "Brain of Katipunan"—authored the (revolutionary) Katipunan's teachings that "all people are created equal." All revolutionaries subscribed to that thought. The IFI/PIC was the remaining vehicle of the Filipino cry and subscribed to that truth, stated in its belief that "we are all created equal, children of God."

The ECUSA helped the PIC to be part of the family to work together for the Kingdom of God, to be seen in the world map, and to be connected with those nationalistic Catholics (not Roman). It celebrated the unity in the Kingdom work and promoted service to life, respect of human dignity, justice and peace, integrity of creation, and more. Unity is celebrated with the realization that independent experience in the struggle for life is a revealing aspect of the way we are. God is glorified with truth that sets people free. Celebrate God as the answer to all our imperfections.

Some of IFI's Sources of Knowledge and Statement of Belief

To address the question about how do IFI know what they know, let me draw some phrases from the basic material available: The Iglesia Filipina left the Romanist Church because of Romanist's "separation from the spirit of Christianity" after they allied themselves (if not pushing it to be) to the cruelty of the racist colonial regime. The IFI did not depart from the Catholic and Apostolic belief. As it said earlier, "Only the Roman Church was wrong, not the Christian religion."

From initial teachings of IFI seen in its fundamental epistle offers teachings to give glimpse of what they were thinking. Some encouraging statement for IFI members to stand even in their lonely journey is reflected its Epistles: 1) "We go our way with our spirits fixed on God'—(Epistle 11). Here, IFIs are willing to move on even in its lonely path while Romanist and Protestants in the Philippines were beating the drum of American imperialism. 2) "To restore the worship of the one true God in all its splendor, and the purity of His most Holy Word" (Epistle 111). "True God" is not a god of *inequality* against "inferiors" but of love. The Church as representing God must promote *love* as the reason of God in sending Jesus to this world, where He preached brotherhood of all people. 3) "Give the faithful the immortal and unique book of God, the Bible" (Epistle 111). Isabelo de los Reyes Sr. cofounder of IFI translated the New Testament into Ilocano, affirmed that the IFI believed the Bible to be understood by ordinary people (together with liturgy of worship into the language of the local people). The Bible or Gospel is believed to be the liberating truth of God where they based their teachings about freedom, love, equality, and brotherhood of all races. 4) "Let them understand the Holy Scripture in all its purity" (Epistle 111). The IFI saw the importance of knowing knowledge taught from the Bible. The core teaching for life must be affirmed in their experience in history and the death of co-Filipinos by selfish appetite of their foreign ruler. The very description of the Bible says "All Scripture is God-breathed and is useful for teaching, rebuking, correcting and training in righteousness" (2 Tim.3:16). What is the meaning of it if 'rebuking and correcting' is outside (has nothing to do with) the human *actual experiences* of Filipinos that provided the reasons why the Bible is relevant to life, and it make sense to life. Take this for example as representing the pro-American evangelicals Charles Swindoll in the Radio for Life station, (May 2, 2011) saying that 'experience should not influence our interpretation of the Bible'. Of course he is from imperialist America. I understood it as good utterance because 'experience' to Americans is different from the oppressed people of the Philippines. Yes, Biblical interpretation should not be influenced or used by imperialistic mode, but should be life sustaining *breath of God* to the oppressed people particularly Filipinos. This was true to 1902 Filipino situations. 5) "Reserve the center of all altars for the symbol of the Trinity" (Epistle 111). The IFI is true to its Trinitarian faith, true to ordinary members of IFI, even during the time when there were crisis with regards to Unitarianism in some few years until Bishop De los Reyes Jr. 6) "We have the same beliefs as Roman Catholic except only obeying the injustices and the error of the Papacy" (Epistle IV). 7) "The same ecclesiastical offices existing in and recognized by the Roman Church shall be conferred" (1902 Constitution of the PIC). 8) "The dogma and creed shall be the same as all the Apostolic Catholic Christians" (1902 Constitution of the PIC). More can be read about IFI's beliefs found in some early documents. The early IFI-documents can show that the basic Christian belief of the IFI has not changed from the faith of "One, holy, Catholic and apostolic."

IFI as totally free from pro-imperialist exploitation—to befriend nationalistic independent churches of independent republics is inevitable. Issue if life always a call for ecclesial existence and brotherhood among others beyond protectionism of exclusivist institution.

What is the depository of knowledge that IFIs know about Christianity? Based on how I learned religious stuff from my boyhood till now in IFI and observed our religious life and teachings in lectures and in theological seminaries, this is how we know what we know: 1) Ecclesiastical (Church) history: One basic source of our knowledge in theological seminaries is the record or history on how this Christian movement started, struggled to survive, struggled in persecution from Jesus to early fathers, from Jerusalem to tolerance of Constantine to the whole world, and to the present WCC movement. History shows how generations exercised their faith, dealt with problems in the darkness done by the threatened powerful empire, and how Christian church divided and hijacked because of it, and how Christians respond to preserve the Church of Christ, etc. 2) Church (Divine) traditions: Before anything else, traditions were there as the life and basis of their beliefs, keeping them united, "passing on the teaching of the Apostles, fellowship, breaking of bread, and in prayer" (Acts 2:42). All of these are seen in our worship and ecclesial life now. 3) Scripture: As early Christians were persecuted, oral traditions must be put in writing, so that now became one book as our present Bible. The Bible is the compilation of all collected writings. Scripture is not one thesis or one set of dogmas as some falsely asserted, but God's biography in dealing with *not perfect* but forgiven people whom He loved in different time and space. It as to be noted that the Bible is not the founder of the Church, but the Church is the producer of it. We have the Bible because we have Church—not otherwise. It should keep us together in Christ's pro-people/life intentionality, instead of dividing us in it with doctrinal positioning that misses the pro-people point of Jesus. God exists not because authors in the Bible say so, but because the Bible tried to state the reality of unfathomable God in dealing with people using the terms available in their different time and situations. 4) Councils: Since controversies or problems cannot be avoided in people, these were created to clarify problems and issues in the Christian faith and straighten any confusion that caused problems, and where to formulate standard of Christian belief. The Councils of Jerusalem and Nicaea took place so that the standard of belief created an answer to the confusions brought by Judaizer (in the council of Jerusalem) and then Gnosticism/Arianism (in the council of Nicaea). 5) Creeds. The standard, stand, or statement of Christian belief is the result of Councils—the Apostles' and Nicene Creeds. These creeds are about one Trinitarian belief realized by the whole Church from the Bible that needs to be emphasized so that problems will not be repeated, and so respected by the Church since nearly two thousand years ago. 6) National experience (or local history of the people): Local or national history should not be ignored. We learned through local history how the nationalistic struggle came into being and how the nationalistic Catholic birthed it. National history also tells us that by imperialistic motives it pushed to "deformity" affecting the image of the Church; that, within the forces of imperialism, it brought changes of the shape and forms of the Church, as what we saw under *patronato real* and pro-imperialist forces of the late nineteenth-century American Protestants. In local history, we found Thomas Jefferson (of the USA), Emilio Jacinto and IFI (in the Philippines) needed to emphasize the teaching "we are all created equal in eyes of God" because of the elements in the ruler of the world that forgets. Those who experienced the opposite felt tasked to bring this into light—and add to that light.

Those above (1–5) are not tickets/permits to abuse life of other human race/being (of color) in aspiring for prestige/power, political and economic gain, in the spirit/sin of racism. Conduct of injustices against other races demonstrated man's actual belief (within the Church) against (Filipino) life. Local history is not a record of how they depart, but to restore what Christianity is all about in relation to love, life, and light of the Lord. We manifest the beauty of man in our reaction against evils, and yet we have the ability to preserve what is to be preserved—the very belief of Historic Apostolic Christianity.

The basis of Christian beliefs followed by IFI is also seen in the IFI Church seal (logo) that reads Scientia, Libertas, Caritas, Scripturae. 1) Scientia or Reason: IFI is with history and historical experience not imprisoned with naiveté for one colonial agenda but *learned* man from the man-made selfish darkness to lift up the Light for life. She is gifted (in mind, heart, emotion, and will) to reason why human beings should be respected and be allowed to grow in full capacity as humans liberated and educated by the truth and teachings of Christ; and that man should naturally react against injustices and suppressions of natural flow of human spirit toward living as "living being" breathed by God. Free man must articulate and give reason to be human. No amount of lies and deceptions should interrupt what human as breathed by God can achieve. Nationalistic Catholics have reasons to exist, to be nationalistic and yet catholic, to be instruments of God to guard the "image of God" in man that the product of what he do points the glory of God, not the glory of one (imperialist) nation or one race (which if we are not watching, Church can be hijacked to serve the isms of the anti-God).

Filipino naiveté (caused by church and political alliance) is one stronghold of the Romanists or imperialists. Man's history is not without learned sensitivity. To live with reasons to share is natural to the learned man who experienced darkness. Only by the bondage of deceptions by religion wanting to please the giant ruler and as itself is imperialist—that man can pretend (if not victimized) that Christianity is all about claims or doctrines. But God is not imprisoned by man's deception and lies.

St. Augustine stated, "For God is a kind of artist whose greatness in His masterpieces is not lessened in His minor works … but only by reason of the wisdom of their Designer."[138] He said, "The great majority of those in heaven preserve the integrity of their nature; and not even the sinfulness of a will refusing to preserve the order of its nature can lessen the beauty of God's total order, designed, as it is, according to the laws of His justice."[139]

2) Libertas or Liberty and freedom is expressed or dictated through actual experience (in injustices, inhuman, lies, and racism) that man naturally aims to achieve if it is denied. Liberated man can do naturally good things that point to worship of God. It is necessary to point out that freedom and liberty are gifts from God. After the sadness of slavery, it is a joy to celebrate the lordship of God. "Brother, you have been called to liberty" (Gal. 5:13) (as IFI Epistle emphasized). This is an essential part of salvation, Jesus has come "to proclaim release for prisoners and restore liberty to the oppressed" (Lk 4:18). "But there is liberty, and the Bible gives no definition. It does, however, at least affirm implicitly that man is endowed with the power of responding by a free choice to God's plans for him. Above all, it shows the path of genuine freedom. Yahweh intervenes, in the OT, to assure the liberation of His people. In the NT, the grace of Christ brings the freedom of the children of God to all men."[140]

3) Caritas or Love and Charity: C. S. Lewis said, 'Charity is love.' Love for other people is the very teaching of our Lord; it is

where "law and the prophets hang on," as Paul said, "the summary" of all the command is love. Love is the fulfillment of the will of God to be celebrated in life, the action of our Christian preaching, realization of the general purpose in Jesus' command is a blessing to those in need, it is about doing service to those least of all humans.

In 1902, H. G. Wells published his racial utopian *New Republic* which is described by some thinkers as a "shocking illustration" (which seems to be saying and actualized in the spirit of imperialism).

And how will the New Republic treat the inferior races? How will it deal with the black? The yellow man? The Jew? Those swarms of black, and brown, and dirty-white, and yellow people, who do not come into the new needs of efficiency? Well, the world is world, and not a charitable institution, and I take it they will have to go … And the ethical system of these men of the New Republic, the ethical system which will dominate the world state, will be shaped primarily to favor the procreation of what is fine and strong bodies, clear and powerful minds … And the method that nature followed hitherto in the shaping of the world, whereby weakness was prevented from propagating weakness … The men of the New Republic … will have an ideal that will make the killing worth the while.[141]

This utopian idea seems to be what is actually experienced by Filipinos; it should be the primary thing that Church should prevent to happen to human race.

Man's weakness or backwardness, if we call it so, may be caused by their religious paganism. It is still in them from the olden days and is seen in how they respect nature and creatures. Maybe we need to learn from them to alter the greediness evident in our time. We propagandize against paganism. We are for Jesus and for life as we say, but behind it is an imperialist spirit that cannot deny or hide from being shocking to us.

4) Scripture is in the IFI logo because it hangs or holds our response and aspirations after the horrifying reality of the time. Scripture is the official book canonized by early Christians and affirmed in the councils. IFI believed that this should be respected as well as the Church Council achievements. What we profess should be affirmed by it. Religions can claim as many as they want, but IFI believed in the order affirmed in this Christian book. It contains the liberating truth of the Messiah, understood by the Filipinos. The Bible contained the core teachings for the reign of God's salvation (from man-made darkness). It contained the very heart of the message of God's love for people and life—embracing all, regardless of color. The life-giving breath for brotherly relationship and order under God's fatherhood is defined in it. "All Scripture is God-breathed and is useful for teaching, rebuking, correcting, and training in righteousness" (2 Timothy 3:16). Victims of inhumanities and unjust evils must find home with it.

The actions of world imperialists contradict the true Christian spirit seen by nationalistic Churches like IFI. Imperialism is offensive to the right and human reason, liberty, charity, and the Bible are not are defense for the offense. Christianity is indeed an action for life (which is affirmed by prolife and anti-imperialist movements at the time it was established).

Some new Christian Fundamentalists looked at it. It seems helpful that imperialists believed that the only source of Christian knowledge is the Bible. They repeat the problems of interpretations already settled in the early historic councils. Early problem groups like Judaizers and Gnosticism somehow helped the early Christians. Because of them, Christians created clarity after those councils. But to remain Bible-centered and dogma-centered, it created divisions and confusions because the Church's relevance to life in search for order in everyday journey is a must. The harmful reality kept giving reasons for divisions or schism (with chapter/verse), so that they became the producers of irrelevant sects. The blinded created more blindness.

American Fundamentalist congregations tried to ignore the achievements of the early Church. What is going to happen then is that in them anyone can claim to have a direct message "given by God" (which is in many cases scriptural abuse). The favorite message is about the Second Coming, End of the World, and anything friendly to the dominant, powerful interest of imperialism. These heaven/end time and prosperity focused congregations, known by their *selective literalism*, cause the small, chopped congregations to be sustained by their "giving" from congregants. It is generally a Christianity of *nicety* that does not encourage critical thinking in the midst of materialist culture. But with the IFI lens, we say, while we are to please God we ought to serve life in this broken world. Life is a measure of our Christian exercise while we intensify our relationship with God.

Romanist and Imperialist Persecution Affecting IFI

The Romanist church favored the unfair 1898 Treaty of Paris because of the desired protection and prestige within the new imperial power of America. One obligation of the United States as a result of this treaty was to protect the Romanist Catholic's properties in the Philippines. In 1906, the US-controlled Philippine court ordered the return of the church buildings brought by Filipinos as they affiliated as PIC. One example of this was in Lagonoy, Camarines Sur.[142] Buildings were claimed by Filipinos became IFIs due to the claim that these were built by their fathers through forced labor. The Romanist desire for property protection is more powerful than submission to the justice of the loving Father that blesses life (supposedly the Church's primary business). This was a defining moment. It caused the Filipinos to ask whether these two winners were really God believers or God users. God appeared to be anti-Filipino, according to their representation who opposed the inequality, racism, and injustice. It is like God is one-sided, pro-materialist, pro-market, and racist at the same time (if that is what the church represented). But no, their conduct was the opposite manifestation of God. It absolutely cannot represent God who loved all people, and Jesus who died for all. It ignored the fallen lives of those who fought for freedom from sin and injustice for a hundred years, showing numbness against the invaded "Christian and civilized nation." This tells us that they became mockers of Christianity. Actions demonstrated the actual belief to god who sanctioned unjust, unfair deeds. Deceptions, lies, and injustices were instruments for their own racial successes. This was not of God because God's purpose brings lasting peace based on justice for all people. The very message of God's love in Jesus is the only sure representation—not anger and hatred as a result of the spirit of racist appetites and greedy deeds. God's truth will ask justice as a payment of the debtors in the end. The justice of God will prevail naturally and absolutely—no one can get away from it. There is vindication of God's truth in actual human situations. As I converse about it, one said, "It boils down to God."

IFI-Filipino's Embrace of Catholicism

IFI is not Romanism but within the Catholic faith. Its love for the catholic faith is not as in the Romanist concept as they understood it (the term "catholic" has two meanings). The original concept comes from the Nicene Creed (promulgated by the Council of Nicaea, used in Eastern as well as Western Christendom). Though Romanists were fond of playing between two meanings, IFI found itself standing on what the term really is in One Holy Catholic and Apostolic Church.

When Romanists confess, "I believe in one holy Catholic" from the Creed, they meant what the early Church was saying (including the Orthodox-Eastern Churches). The statement of belief was not created for the Romanist Church, but for the (undivided) whole Christian Churches gathered in the Council of Nicaea.

The reality of evil darkness caused some religious nationalism in different nations (including IFI), but they are not anti-Catholic. Romanists were using the creed to preserve unity, ignoring the cry of the human heart brutalized by colonial era. The creed had a secondary meaning by them; they said "believing in *one* (under Papal headship) … *catholic* (Roman Catholic)." The secondary meaning that they can play around is undeclared change of meaning, but assumed by followers. Their understanding now of the word "catholic" can be said to be stolen by the Romanists.

Perhaps IFI can offer some preservation of the real meaning, coming from its very heritage. "Catholic" means universal, inclusive, beyond colors, interracial in Christ, and all children of God. Romanist Vatican-Papal-centered catholicity may sound dominant and loudly oppressive, but the truth of the term is not determined by the survival of the fittest mentality. Catholicity is *not* owned by the Romanists. Christian catholicity is about Messiah's mission "for God so loved the whole people." Those that believe will be given the right to become children of God (see Jn. 1 and 3:16). IFI taught the wisdom of the truth after what was revealed in their struggle in history. Catholicity is for inclusiveness of all races and the universal message of the love of God—not the exclusiveness by the claimant Rome. To receive Christ qualifies all to be children of God—coheirs with the Lord Jesus. IFI Epistle teaches that all are children of God. Churches who knew that we should respect the history of race must blow the trumpet of the needs so that we can go back to the table and talk of going back to the original concept of catholicity. Orthodox Churches surely will welcome the conversation for a new era of United Church for God's kingdom on earth that blesses all, in all, and for all.

V
Honest Reflections for the Table Talk and for the Ecclesiality of Life

When Freedom Became Unpleasant to Their Ear

Who viewed freedom as a *threat*? In the early years of settlement from England, Americans viewed freedom as a sweet word to say as an expression of truth and the gift of life. When America became imperialist (by Republicans) after its final invasion of the Philippines in 1902, that same word became a *bad* word to the imperialists. The situation changed the understanding!

During the years of implementation of America's Sedition Law (in the Philippines), no one was allowed to say "freedom." It could cost their lives for anyone who would say it. The new nature of the nation became imperialist and naturally changed the way they heard the sound and meaning of it to become like a bad, irritating, threatening word. So that now, when you hear "freedom, freedom, freedom" from the imperialist's mouth, you hear hypocrisy. Freedom is theirs against the invaded and ruled subjects. Of course, America's anti-imperialist group, years before the anti-flag law, addressed the wrong done to the nation that the Philippine flag represents. The major anti-imperialist arguments said it clearly. Imperialism in general and annexation in particular contradicted American ideals. Democrat Presidential candidate William Jennings Bryan said, "The fruits of imperialism, be they bitter or sweet (for Americans) ... It is the voice of the serpent, not the voice of God that bids us eat."[143]

The *Liberation Theology* by the Roman Church is truly meaningful only if should repent about the abuse and sins committed to Filipino people during the bad episode of ecclesial history during colonial era by encomenderos and friars. If it is not, then the said freedom or liberation is just one dishonest-bait of religious deception for the weak or naïve humans, a hypocrisy pinning the name of God —while advancing the uncompromising interest of monopoly.

Is this about playing life for selfish power? It is sad that it is still the Roman imperialist way (absolutely not the way of Jesus) for the kingdom of imperialism (not for God's Kingdom). Now if Romanist Church discourages members to believe what liberation theology is all about (as is now happening in many places in Latin America, if not the whole Romanist Catholic), no wonder, because by implication, liberation theology became a continuous call to confession of the Church's sins, served as judgment to their own actions that needs a verdict in the end—a shame and sin that must be confessed.

In 1994, Pope John Paul II confessed the sins of the Romanist Church committed during the colonial era as its "dark side of history."[144] *Time* magazine stated, "The Day of Pardon on March 12, 2000, a ritual presided over by Pope John Paul II and meant to purify two millenniums of church history. In the presence of wooden crucifix that had survived every siege of Rome since the fifteenth century, high-ranking Cardinals and bishops stood up to confess the sins against indigenous peoples, women, Jews, cultural minorities, and other Christians and religions."[145] So it did really happen as confessed!

By implication, Dr. Jose Rizal's contention in *Noli Me Tangere*, regarding the Romanist Church abuses (through royal patronage and friars) was again confirmed by it, and Archbishop Bernardino Nozalida's rebuke of *Noli Me Tangere* is purely part of a political game. The question is how sincere was the confession if the Romanist has no capacity to recognize the importance, reasons, or meaning of the Nationalist Churches—a product of struggle for equality, inclusive love, justice and freedom, particularly of the Iglesia Filipina Independiente? Their antagonism to nationalist churches (especially IFI) is still evident in *The Catholic Encyclopedia*, showing how they picture the IFI or Anglicans or Episcopals.

Romanist dogmatism seems more powerful than pro-freedom and pro-love that is supposedly the spirit of Christianity. It sustains the spirit of darkness by that as it lost its ability to truly, honestly repent regarding its previous assaults to human dignity, violating the real purpose of the gospel of Jesus and the Church to Filipinos in the era of Patronato Real, encomienda, and Friarocracy of Friars, as the final authority of the local Roman Catholic Church was given to the monarch as Royal Patron.

Infallibility as One Idea for Eternal Solution

Papal Infallibility claims that the pope cannot make a mistake in what he pronounces in his ex cathedra—the "pope cannot be wrong" kind of dogma. This is a Romanist instrument to "eternal solution" for oneness or ecclesial unity if problems occur. This kind of Papal power affected his decision whether it was worth listening to the Filipino case against Friars' abuses (before 1899) in the Philippines. "Infallibility is just one idea," said an ex-Romanist priest. I thought this idea should not represent the Church of Christ as a whole for one selfish intention—and it must not be a final revelation in life as they may label other groups who are displaying ideas or actions that are not necessarily agreeable to the Romanists.

The power of the infallible head contributed the ignorance of the fact that truth of life of the Filipino race demonstrated in history is an instrument of understanding their humanness. Church ruled by an infallible head is limiting itself the ability to see by the dictates of institution, council, and dogma, so that the truth to be uncovered is limited to what pleases the political party. So "idea-church" of infallibility may ignore the facts of human struggles, may rewrite history to serve the instrument RC institution, and may make propaganda history, not taking seriously the struggle of people as in Filipino grievances.

The struggle and reality of life of the powerful subject can result in another spiritual vessel (another church such as IFI) as a product of the Christian hearts obeying his character. As we know, the institutional infallible "church of idea" should be defensive. How can that not contradict the message that *the truth shall set you free* if that truth is a threat? Dogma of infallibility in IFI's thinking is good only if humans are counted for dogma only. But we are human, obeying the nature that we are created and acted in history against his oppressor. Humans are capable of defining himself in which Church must help in understanding the honest nature.

Nationalist IFI points to the heart, mind, emotion, soul, and understanding reflective of the Creator. The oppressors seems to have *deprived* themselves to understand feelings or emotion that the other races had; seems they build callosity in which not the design or "order" of God. IFI is a mark of human response in the midst of struggle for dignity. IFI is a group of people of different experiences, different issues of struggle, different groups, different places, and different dialects that became one in one issue for respect of life based on God.

What is disturbing is that by cowardice power of infallibility, we are giving the impression to the world that "truth" is defined not by honest actuality of facts, but by assertion of things no matter how wrong may be, infallible head settles it, or no matter how untrue, the pronounced "truth" is final. If "truth" is created by it, then everyday reality/truth is not counted for "setting us free." Seems like American fundamentalist have the attitude of being "already in heaven" so that everyday facts don't matter anymore.

To Be under God as the Way to Order

There are fanatical sectarians antagonistic to IFI (preaching in streets, in radio programs, in proselytizing efforts) based on lies and false claims, thinking that IFI is just one church participated in the competition and religious experiments without spiritual conviction (shaped by her historical sense); No revealing importance operates in it because its interest is to attract people in the world of the contest/ fittest mentality. Those sect/fundamentalist seemed incapable of seeing the Godly wisdom revealed in IFI—those sectarians looked at IFI as what these fundamentalist really were (group of popularity contest of the 'fittest' game).

The one who forced himself to be detached from the presence of God thinks that history does not count for making sense of the Christian religion. It covers his conscience with religious imperialist agenda. He cannot see the wisdom revealed in the depth of IFI as a manifestation of God who breathed upon the living being in creating the total human. Dwelling in a popularity contest that is served by propaganda and lies (in which IFI is one victim) seems to push God away.

On the other hand, should Church power be determined by number of people? So that you have this bargaining power to be blessed by the "powerful" nation? It seems that fear of power and the panic response for securing that position is ruining the very purpose of God! Jesus said, "Those who want to be first should be last. Those who want to be great must be the servant of all." A man or an institution's greatness must be used now to serve the purpose of God and people on earth; if you are 'first' be the servant to promote life. Jesus said, "Why do you call me 'Lord, Lord,' and do not do what I say? (Lk 6:46). Winners should not do the opposite, but must discover the godly wisdom and stand for it.

We read history books to know what actions and what equivalent reactions man can get. Then we ask, "Is this what really life is all about?" When actions produce reactions, there is *learning*. But if we continue to ignore the cry for one uncompromising selfish agenda, it becomes a force to think different from the design, a force to ignore the emotion and feelings, a force to deny man in his full capability to build a loving environment, and to love and to believe another human to work for the common good.

In *To Serve the Devil*, Paul Jacob and others stated, "The history of American expansionism is directly linked to American racism. Almost every instance of armed intervention has been undertaken against a colored people including Latin Americans … the theme of racism emerges more clearly. Zion in the Wilderness, Manifest Destiny, The American Mission, The American Century, all represent visions of a white American that rules the world; dreams for an empire."[146] All should see the evil dark results and learn from the actual outcome revealed in the stage of actions of the combat field so we can learn to serve life. Ask if it is of God or of the devil.

If the Church aimed to promote those visions, praising the actions of imperialism, it seems detached from Jesus. We all should realize and recognize that God's truth means love, life, respect, freedom, justice, and peace. We got war, terrorism, climate change, famine, cultural revolutions, economic agenda, etc. This seems to be a hundred years of tribulations (1898 to present). The century of world wars for economic reasons, arrogance and pride, should lead everyone to look at the beautiful plan of God in man and woman then we should glorify the Lord who has the beautiful purpose for life and for this only earth.

Many individuals will not do anything but pretend to be blind, unthreatened by the ways of the world. Has no ability to preserve life, deciding to be nice to preserve the family bridging them to the next era. But preserving *status quo* for the next era that cannot preserve life is a waste of opportunity.

Catholicity by Nationalistic and Historical is Life-Centered

One author said, "There is one Cultural Christianity (Romanist) and another is Authentic Christianity." I'm afraid that the second limits God as moralist. Authentic means "born again" or fundamentalist conservative type. We pray it should not. Moralistic view is one attraction of the many to be counted as authentic. If being authentic and moralistic means you do not smoke, dance, and drink alcohol, we are using big words for cheap talk about a small god. It can break our heart if the end of Christian talk is limited only to not smoking, feeling good, and speaking in tongues to earn be labeled authentic. There will be much heartbreak if this makes them confident enough to be making and empowering naiveté, incapacitating Christians to see the immorality (politically and socially) by the leaders pushing for unjust and illegal war, enabling the policy for the purposes of isms— no matter how much this can ruin the lives and home of innocents (just because what they care is that kind of "authenticity").

Nationalistic Catholic's Christianity is a life-centered Christianity of God. This is all of the above because culture and morals should serve the purpose of life and people. What is being cultural but escaping against the people's history and experience and its lessons of the past, or being authentic but allied to the global social Darwinist, and materialist imperialism that can treat life lesser than the interest of market-driven assertion?

Only through life-centered Christianity can we bring Christianity-centered life (not materialist centered), not that life is separated from direct issue of life/people, or that God is not our help to seek order for our life on earth ruined by selfish isms. Life is God-breathed and we cannot take Him away from where we are. This is why Jesus makes us realize the truth of it.

Take climate change and 'ignoring environmental demands,' or corruption and human trafficking as serious threats to life. Of course, our call is to *change* our ways of life in which our national government is one effective agent for the change. Whatever happens in our situation by man's making, in the end, it should cause everyone to look back to God and His good purpose in life. We should realize that man is operating independently from the will of God. He must evaluate what he is worshipping and what is his god. On the other hand, it is not right for the claimers of authentic Christianity to jump in and proclaim his personal Lord and personal Savior and say you cannot blame God for our environmental problems because this is none of His business! No, God can point us back to our stewardship of creation (Genesis 2:15), unless you think He is totally useless for social good.

Cultural Christianity may beat the drums for cultural fiestas. Authentic Christians can bind God away from life in political issues while looking up to heaven for hope and rapture. Life-centered Christians should be watching the directions or walk of people's lives. The kind of Church-shaped ecclesiality is to be truthful to the very prophetic task. God is for life and people and so must be our type of Christianity.

(Though the promises of heaven cannot be changed just because you are not obsessed with it or because you think more of how you can please God in the darkened world, more than being expert of the scriptural text that promises heaven. The Lord in the judgment/last day to act as Judge will give justice to whom justice is due, including those who didn't expect for heaven or not fixated about being in the right hand or who will be in the left).

Nationalistic Catholicism Must Be Birthed for the New Concept of Order

The Gospel of John talks about the time of Jesus. It says "Darkness came into the world." The old Roman imperialism was anti-freedom, causing racial chaos and hatred. Jewish people became divided because of their presence, and religious sects—Pharisees and Sadducees—benefited its power. The Jewish religious system was corrupted (Lk 3:1–2), but the time was right for the salvation of God through the Messiah. "By the government of heathen, which the Jews were under, to show that they were conquered people, and therefore it was time for the Messiah to come to set up a spiritual kingdom."[147]

During the twentieth century in the Philippines, religious Roman Catholics and American Evangelical Protestants served as instruments of the new empire of capitalism. The truths of the Messiah's teaching must be embraced by the conquered, and must be grasped and affirmed as the hope of the oppressed (or victims) Filipinos. That to receive and believe Him will have Life—to open the heart for Him and to submit to his Truth, to yield upon his teachings and pro-life/people commandments. Apostle John said that generation, and for all of us that "receive him, to those who believed in his name, he gave the right to become children of God" (Jn 1:12). This is what IFI's catholicity is all about.

Many in today's generation regarded the Church (in general) as a place where hypocrisy dwells. They point back to the pages of Patronato Real, Laissez-Faire, Manifest Destiny, and the actions of Spanish friars and American religious. True, sects became *justifiers* and *pacifiers* even if it meant death to the poor and weak nations and people. Ruins cause chaos for the advantaged to rule. It is believed therefore that all Christians should aim to restore the true image of the Church.

The Nationalist Church is going to restore the concept of catholicity away from the oppressive exclusivist hand. For the Church must serve the essentials of Jesus, which is the Kingdom of God in which He is obeyed as Lord and King (see Lk 4:43; Jn 18:37). If Romanist's catholicity is about global headship centered to Rome (concerning control and uniformity), PIC's catholicity is of the Father to his children whom he loved. This catholicity by implication is concerning freedom, love, justice, righteousness, and respect for human dignity, centered to Jesus Christ as the Way, Truth, and Life; and the Light of the world (Jn 14:6; 8:12).

When the Philippine islands were invaded by Americans in 1899, it was already civilized and Christianized. The Philippine invasion indeed was unfit for McKinley's reasoning. What kind of culture would be introduced and be offered better than what Filipinos knew that time? But if conquering the Philippine nation is just because they could do it, kill the defenders of freedom even though not angry or mad, then Mark Twain was right when he suggested for the American flag a 'symbol of death under the banner of skull and crossbones.'

Now, though this IFI/PIC is a nationalist and independent (as many historical churches arose with other nations' struggles). In terms of Kingdom work, they believed that this was not a monopoly of one. All races in independent nationalist political experiences are part (not an enemy/threat to be ignored) of the catholicity of God's love for all, centered to Christ.

An oppressive church of control needs to have visible, absolute power, infallible headship centered to one place Rome. The deepest pain of struggle of the victimized people were not regarded as important as revealing aspects of the divine design in human with the highest goal of success for freedom—paying with blood and lives. Romanist and American Churches seems became incapable of seeing this because what matters was their concept of order—no matter how this served as a disordering factor in the Christian world. It shows that pro-imperialists let go of the capacity to see the beauty of God's purpose and wisdom capable of building the lasting peace in an equally loving world. It seems to please the *Pax Americana/Pax Romana* (serving "order" according the rule of imperialism).

God's message for life was seen and understood and embraced as more important for the people who longed for it (represented by IFI). They rose from its ashes and ruins. Now felt tasked to share the message for the new world order of life based on justice and peace of God, His truth that must be heard, reflecting our basic reasons why we longed for God amid the success of (man's) selfish and arrogance over territory and materialist agendas. That order may be caused by God—not in terms of Bibliolatrous dogmatism—as a cry of the poor and oppressed human heart, now freed, educated, and liberated in the teaching of Christ. Church nationalism—as the product or result of pro-people endeavors against the actions by the ungodly—must be one instrument to see the human nature that points to one architect or designer of human being.

There are products of influence of the conquering culture. Some sectarian (entrepreneur) churches can be called killers of Church. One group wanted to end the Orthodox, which was embraced by the Greek-speaking Christians. They said, "Outside of the Roman Church, there is no salvation." That salvation was their monopoly and infallibility is awarded to them (watch out because American-born fundamentalists are having their own infallibility too, claiming that they have pipe of God's voice from heaven now, seems pushing the yesterday's Bible as obsolete. What a divisive and Christian destruction that culture brings without a chance of healing).

One church seems to be stealing the religious name like "Church of Christ" or "Iglesia Ni Cristo" from the Bible and used it as the title of their group or church. They claimed to be legitimate Christians because the title of their church is in the Bible, and that others must be wiped out and be eliminated because their name like Iglesia Romana, Orthodox or Anglican, or Iglesia Filipina are not found in the Bible. That's what they taught by example, doctrinism/dogmatism outside the breath taking experience in history of the victimized souls. It is sad to say that individuals tend to do the same—killing the usefulness of others against the Kingdom work because of the culture of doctrine-ism. They claim to focus outside of man's historical sense. Because of ignorance of the supporters of this kind of entrepreneurial church, now, the whole Church is reduced into a popularity contest. That kind of attitude is not endorsed by the Bible and harms the Church (of Christ).

In a *popularity contest*, some believed that *truth* only belonged to those who have the capacity to create them. Brain washing, lies, claims, media, monopoly, display power, propaganda, and biased history became essentials to attract people. They are not historically grounded, so human struggle for justice and respect for human dignity is not part of the language of the Kingdom. Is God's message or Church irrelevant to ordering our lives on earth?

Relying on the *ways of the world* is giving the Church a bad name. Popularity contests causing others to think that Church is just about number of adherents and power to protect that number. Sadly, many negative thoughts we can hear now say that Church/ Christianity is just about religion and hypocrisy, focusing on minor issues and immoralities (smoking, drunkenness), and neglecting the big and real immoralities like unjust war, lies, deception, murdering of innocents, human rights violation, false promises, public lying as "there are weapons of mass destruction." The cowardly powers ruined the civilizations of 'weak' poor countries, leave them or force them to serve the interests of the powerful giants.

Some thought of Church as for special interest only—and not to serve life. To aim for territorial and political ally, seek blessings from imperialist power, employing lies and claims, peer pressure in schools and work places, etc. seems separated from very purpose of Christ. It is one manifestation of insecurities, not about God at all.

The IFI Epistle taught about schisms. "Schismatic are not we … for a schismatic is not one who separates from the pope but one who separates from God, from his justice, and from the purity of

His word" (Epistle IV). No one can do wrong against other people unless you are separated from His love and justice. Revolution may not be if all hearts are faithful to the purpose of God. Church is not about position, wealth, and idolatry to the powerful. It is true that power and prestige can be good instruments for the Ministry, but they are bad if they become the master. The Roman Church ends up protecting and securing it, causing the Orthodox Church to think it is impossible to reconcile with.

The Issue of Life Matters the Most

The issue of life is the theme of this Nationalist Church (even in the whole Anglican families), rather than the issue of universal uniformity, political positioning, and creating absolute power according to the concept or ways of the world. How hurting it seems to the pro people principles of God for the "Church" to actually serve as the connivance of imperialism for power for global-economic interest and for wealth that demoralizes the weak nations.

We should know by the fruit (displayed conduct) who is the blesser of what. In the issue of life and death (in the 1902 Philippines, for example), you teach things *away* from the issue of life? Know by then who is your lord? Is the one in the Bible or the Bible itself (for dogmatism, or pretext for claims)? We got to have the heart of Jesus working in the heart of man, not callous hearts in the midst of bloodshed and injustice. It is very unlikely for the Church to be a *blesser* of the unjust, deceptive, liar, or invader at that time. By it, the church invalidated and invalidates more the Messiah Jesus and his teachings about his love, will, and the kingdom.

Aggressive US-born fundamentalists, faith/cultic movements, and sects tend to divert the focus from Jesus to the Holy Spirit so that the end of Christianity is to *feel good*. The church can invalidates Christ's teaching like "Love your enemies and pray for those who persecute you" (Mt. 5:44); "Blessed are you who are poor" (Lk 6:20); "If anyone wants to be first, he must be the last, and the servant of all" (Mk 9:35); "Whoever wants to become great among you must be your servant, and whoever wants to be first must be slave of all" (Mk 10:43–44) --if what matters to it is "spirit" (or heaven).

These American faith/cult fundamentalist churches who love very dearly the teaching of miracles only, and psycho-babbling, positive thinking, left behind thinking are churches that tend to divert God with their claims/dogmatism, putting the Bible above what this is for, away from the issue of life; and feel good in the Spirit, joining the circus of spiritual drunkenness, and that's it. They get excited in war and expect it to be called Armageddon. They welcome calamities as a sign of the end of the world—no touch from the actual situation caused by the powerful. They cannot proclaim Jesus as the answer to our problems or relate to Jesus as *liberator*. Men and women of history know the tricks of Romanist friars—this is no different! Is God being mocked? If they think they can play God, they're killing the Church. The alternative then is *self*. Why should one believe then in the Church and waste time and monetary support (which I'm afraid is now the case).

Christianity is *for* life and love. Love is the nature that shows our being disciples. If there is killing and injustice, the first person who gets offended is supposedly the Christian; they should be the first kind of person who supposedly get affected by injustices? The people that should ask what this is? Why kill? Why war? Why use the weak? Why selfish motives? If the Church that focuses more on positive thinking, then in the midst of wrong and illegal wars, you can still preach *victorious positive thinking* and not being bothered by the evils of wars. This is one reason why Joel Osteen is America's favorite! Christianity should be rescued from entertaining as if it is hypnotizing the taxpayers. This is bothersome. We should give and lift up the Light of Christ (as the light of the world) where the man-made darkness is real—in the death of the weak ruined by the intimidation and demoralization of the strong. This is the absolute reason of Christ's word and light for the world.

In the Gospel, we found out about the relationship of God and fellow men—not about spirit. It is not about religion or heaven as the main concern. As Christians, we should start from Christ and His teachings. St. Paul is one good interpreter of them. In Mark 12:29–34, Jesus said, "This is the first and great commandment … There is no other commandment greater than these." We should keep the ranking the way Jesus did. He was talking about God and neighbors—our life on earth. In Matthew 6:33, it said, "Seek ye first the kingdom and His righteousness." It is about life. In John 13:34, "A new commandment I give you: Love one another." This is about man, woman, young, and old.

Jesus taught that the real greatness is about service to people (Mk 10:42–43). St. Paul said "And whatever other commandment there may be, are summed up in this one rule: 'Love your neighbor as yourself.'" Love does no harm to its neighbor. Therefore love is the fulfillment of the law." (Romans 13:9–10). It is about life—here and now. We do not discount that there is life beyond prepared for us—all should be there—but we have to answer what have we done. Jesus said, "I tell you the truth, whatever you did for the one of the least of these brothers of mine, you did it for me" (Mt 25:40). I see the end time in many calamities. It can be our opportunity to find the answer, but the childish say, 'Calamities didn't happen to us because God favored us!'

We can reflect also in the "I am" of Jesus. "I am the bread of life; he who comes to me shall not hunger" (Jn 6:35). "I am the light of the world; he who follow me will not walk in darkness" (Jn 8:12). "He" and the "world" is not about "spirit" and "heaven," but for the darkened world. "I am the resurrection and the life; he who believes in me shall live" (Jn 11:25). This is about believing in Jesus. "I am the way, the truth, and the life" (Jn 14:6). Living closely related to Jesus as the way, truth, life, we do not wait to die to enjoy the truth of these. Eternal life is promised, that is "to know God" (Jn 17: 3) in relationship with Him. We can reflect on His teachings. "Kingdom to come and God's will be done on earth." This does not mean for "heaven of spirits" because this is already done there.

The Bible taught about the "salvation and kingship" of God. Genesis tells us that, after generations, Jacob's family became slaves, but Yahweh saved them from the yoke of the Egyptians (Exodus 6:6). Israelites became people and servants of Pharaoh. Yahweh said, "I will take you as my own people and I will be your God" (v. 7). He was not talking about salvation of "spirit" here. The people of Israel celebrated the feast of the Passover, celebrating Yahweh as their Savior. Isaiah (11) prophesied the coming king and Messiah; this is the salvation of God prepared for all people (Lk 2:30), not all spirit. "He will reign over the house of Jacob forever; his kingdom will never end" (Lk1:33). This is talking about salvation of total man, not spirit after death. The most beloved verse of all, John 3:16, says, "For God so loved the world that He gave his one and only Son, that whoever believes in him shall not perish but have eternal life." The world does not have spirits that will be saved, but they who have Jesus in their hearts who believed. "He is the way, the truth, and the life," is a blessing for the here and now people of God, for the total man, not in spirit only. This is must be said that nationalist Catholic as IFI is not anti-dogma/creed, but pro-life/human first. IFI is not a playful Church with dogma for position, control, and imperialism; thank God that it is not a temptation.

St. James tells as about "the religion that God the Father accepts as pure and faultless is the one who takes care of orphans and widows" (Jas 1:27). Christian life is not about relocation and escape to heaven, but living in this world promoting respect, love, justice, and living as brothers and sisters in Christ. "There is neither Jew nor Greek, slave nor free." We are all one in Christ (Gal. 3:28). It is what we do (as a result of our faith) to people that we are judged whether we go to heaven or hell (Mt 25:31–45).

VI
What Kind of Christianity?
Thoughts for Life Cannot Be Ignored

Where Do Truth and Faith Stand in the Business of Power?

Pastor Pat Robertson quit as head of the Christian Coalition to make President George W. Bush head. *The Washington Post* said, "Pat Robertson's resignation ... as president of the Christian Coalition confirmed the ascendance of a new leader of the religious right in America, George W. Bush. For the first time since religious conservatives became a modern political movement (of America), the president of the United States has become the movement's de facto leader ..."[148]

Atheist Richard Dawkins mentioned that "Bush is Born Again Christian."[149] Today's conservative evangelicals and fundamentalists generally identify themselves as born again Christian (to mean not Catholic or Mainstream Protestant). It is a confusing name being introduced. To show respect to my Christian faith, I must say here that Bush's fabrication of the weapon of mass destruction (WMD) issue is not because he is a Christian. Iraq has different story. His faith about Iraq's WMD is not a representation of being a Christian. It may be as fundamentalist "Born again" (pro-Americanist/imperialist), but not as Christ's Christianity in preserving life and justice even to those who are not Americans. I hold on to this thought as saving the good image of true Christianity.

Fundamentalists (born-again Christians) can go with a dualistic way of thinking, which is scary because two worlds of good and evil is no debate. You must simply take a side to what is good. In the name of good, you will do anything to suppress the evil. No matter what you do and how unacceptable it might be to others, it becomes justifiable in their dualistic world. As the Roman imperialist way (if compare with Jewish experience), Romans attacked the freedom defenders (Zealots) in Masada (Israel). They said that these people were not normal because "normal people don't live at the top of the rock" (as our Pilgrim tour guide said). It is not normal to people, therefore, there is no debate on the two worlds. In normal versus abnormal, normal should win. Good must win over evil! But who is good and who is evil? Who said it? The reality of the picture is that truth suffered when the word is used to justify against the actual truth—instead of giving the honor to free us to enjoy being human. Why lie and kill and claim to be a believer of God? With that, Wikileak's messenger must be silenced because he is delivering the truth (good tool to free the oppressed and oppressor)?

In a radio interview about the Bush administration (KNPR, 9/27/2006), Senator Dianne Feinstein said, "This is the most arrogant administration that I know; I don't want to say it, but it's true." She said, there is no weapon of mass destruction—they say it in the speech: by the president (Bush Jr.), the vice president, and the –secretary of state. That arrogance can be a feeling of the one who thought that he fought for good against evil. But look at the consequences to deception?

The truth of Bush's Iraq war is told (in the book edited by Anita Miller) by Ambassador Joseph C. Wilson. "It is a serious abuse of power that undermines the historic traditions of this country."[150] Serious thinking Americans do not like the idea of betraying the historic tradition or heritage. "There were indications even before September 11, 2001, that President Bush and key members of his administration were fixated on the military invasion of Iraq, regardless of the provocation."[151] As Texas governor, Bush said to Mickey Herskowitz: "One of the keys being seen as a great leader is to be seen as a commander in-chief … My father had all this political capital built up when he drove the Iraqis out of Kuwait and he wasted it … If I have a chance to invade … if I had that much capital, I'm not going to waste it."[152] Herskowitz said that Bush's beliefs about Iraq were based in part on a notion ascribed to now-Vice President Dick Cheney, "Start a small war. Pick a country where there is justification you can jump, go ahead and invade." More is revealed in the book. The justification for it is from fundamentalist religion. The war was an event that the free honest human heart cannot pretend unaffected. Are we to celebrate lies?

Folk rock musicians David Crosby, Graham Nash, Stephen Stills, and Neil Young (CSNY) represent the simple, ordinary-minded people in the business of human concern and justice. They can entertain us with their beautiful blended voices in their songs, but the Iraq War left them no reason to entertain people, but instead a moment to send their message. Truth and sanctity of life cannot be ignored; as informed humans, their hearts cried out. They sang to express the truth of being human and for the truth of human life. These singers of culture made a freedom of speech tour concert about life and justice. They showed their hearts more than those who claimed moralist Christians (fundamentalist) with callous heart (and diverted attention to heaven focusing on praising Bush's action by beating the imperialist drum). The folk rockers sang, "Let's impeach the president for lying and misleading our country into war, abusing the power that we gave him, and shipping all our money out the door." [153] You may Google "Bush deception" and these things are there.

On February 1, 2006, Oprah Winfrey interviewed President George W. Bush with tough questioning about the alleged lies that got the United States into Iraq. Oprah asked, "Your charges about WMD (weapon of mass destruction), you said that was true then. Would you say that today?" Bush answered, "I had documents that supported it … I was speaking to somebody from State. They said that they doubted it happened that way, but that there was a chance that it did."

Oprah said, "This was what I don't get. Because when you were here before, you said that there were about four hundred pages of documents." Bush said, "Absolutely." Oprah continued, "Do you wish you had added a disclaimer?" Bush said, "I don't know if I wish I had offered a disclaimer or if I had just talked about certain events in a different way. I think that would have been the more appropriate thing to do than putting in a disclaimer." Oprah responded, "I appreciate you being here because I believe the truth can set us free. I realize this has been a difficult time for you, and maybe this is the beginning of another kind of truth for you." Bush answered, "I think you're absolutely right.

I mean, I think is obvious—this hasn't been a great day for me. It certainly hasn't been a great couple weeks for me. But I think I come out of it better. I feel like I came here and I have been honest with you. I have, you know, essentially admitted to … [sigh] lying.[154]

Born again fundamentalists must be honest to save the Church from the notion that it worships world power of chance against other humans. No Church should cover the cross with American flags. If they went to war on the basis of arrogance and justified it with lies about weapon of mass destruction, this seriously offensive to the purpose of God! Fundamentalists said, "The Bible is the only book of truth." Anita Miller's contention (and others like Dilip Hiro, Scott McClellan, Bob Woodward, Ron Suskind, etc.) must not be taken seriously? This is seriously a wakeup call for humans. Now, is the father of lies (Satan) surely clapping his hands because in the death of many innocent humans, shows deception as enthroned or empowered by the deceived?

The truth, according to Jesus, shall set us free. Total truth should not be covered, but should be our raw material to point out the goodness of God in life that brings glorification of God, and our human life should celebrate it. Keep the sanctity of truth *sacred* and the greatness of God should be defined and revealed by it. We worship God—not the flag (which is not the intention of the first Americans. George Washington, Jefferson, Madison, and Patrick Henry were Anglicans/Episcopalians that had no intention of creating America as a racial and imperial cult). Jefferson said, "Men were created equal." Still not late, we can have a kind of worship to the Lord of justice in which the whole human race should celebrate, a worship that brings sustainable and lasting peace.

Confusing "God" of Pro Imperialists: Small God of Half-Man's Creation

Playing about two types of "gods" exists in the mind: "small god" and the "big" God. Since there is one perceived small god we must call the real God a Big God who is the God of all truths in man's reality true to his "heart, mind, spirit, soul and strength" a total "living being" (not concerning spirit only) in the world of reality and actuality of man. "Big God" is the answer to the whole, big and total reality of all things here and now (witness of man with history).

But there are "Christians" (detached from their history) seems unconsciously making themselves for spiritual (things of spirit) only and detached all things of God away from this world of struggle; and so consciously or not, they made it or created this kind of small god concept (or god of spirit and heaven only). Now, what is this small god? Simply a product of seems "half-man" (as if can recognize things of spirit only) who thought they are all about in the business of spirit to heaven. They "created" the image of "God" according to man's image (instead of God created them), according to his desired likeness. But Jesus Christ (of God) didn't come to make you and me small and for spirit only, heavenward only, after death only, millennium event only, end time or end of the world only, and Second Coming only, and making us half-man that is fixated to relocate to the second life in heaven. Half-man (spirit only) absolutely is not complete as God designed humans as "living being'" steward of this earth. No, as our Bible taught "all heart, all mind, all soul, all spirit and all strength" is Christ's putting in human language for our reasoning for the motive of incarnated God Emanuel.

134

The truth is that man is created in God's image; he/she is body and spirit complete "living being" (Genesis 2:7). We cannot disregard the whole truth of man as a reflection of God's image and his likeness by creating the "small god" just to please the "global power of the economic world"—to be untouchable by this kind of god—a half-man's creation. The "half god" is naturally smaller than the world's imperialist with global market agenda. Of course we cannot ridiculously reduce God to creating Him. He created us not that we created Him according to the half-man image with limited view of the world. This is seems a big joke but sad.

What seems to be happening in the picture of actuality is that half and small-god is definitely man's creation (in mind). His being half-man is the same product of the image or thought of a coward man wanting to project niceness to please the uncompromising "powerful" idol, which is in so doing, he is making it or adding it to be uncompromising (shielded as "divine"). Confusing, right? Reduced into 'spirit only'—man must think of spiritual and heavenly only, God should be reduced into spiritual only, and the winner is the big (global) imperialist. "Church" by fundamentalism is made a vehicle, at the same time, to serve the powerful giant, but also a vehicle for the making of God. This deception about man and about God must be recognized and be identified in the end to see the glory of God's design. Our motive is about life, not playing game for an imperialist's end, but serious business for life as it was in the beginning.

The idolized "power" of the world is indirectly served by this playing of words about god of half-man's creation; it may appear blessed, watching the success of the making of half-man for their benefits. The incapacitated limited shallow and narrow (as seems it does) mind can fail to see the totality and the depth of reality (in which the total man ought to see the total/whole thing in this world in which the whole human being must engage). The god of half-man's creation is god put in the box and closet of niceness. Half-man controls his/her half god and says, "God concerns spiritual things only," but in his/her discretion he acted as the *boss*. There is really one big mess here: limited god versus total global agenda.

One born again was proud of having little knowledge of the whole situation of the world imperialism, saying what is that political 'none of my business' word? I say, that's it, according to his understanding of himself and God? Don't know and don't want to know the effect of the "worshipped" imperialism, the implication of it, how it became major part of world history and Philippine history, and by what devilish and ruinous means it should be sustained? Don't want to know much about shameful past? Ignorance and naiveté of the citizens is serving as power and strength to wage war in their name, justified by the empowering ignorance. Indeed, play in the success of the anti-life isms.

George W. Bush said to Palestine Prime Minister Mahmoud Abbas, "God told me to strike at Al Qaida and I struck them, and then He instructed me to strike at Saddam, which I did."[155] But you see, God dragged into something work that deceived the president in which Fundamentalist Christians are beating the drums for it. Osama bin Laden was killed in Pakistan, not in Iraq. In one book's cover stated, "The Case for Impeachment lays out the reasons why in a straightforward, letter-of-law manner. Juxtaposing hard facts with the lies and deceptions of this (Bush) administration ..."[156]

Ignorance and naiveté served power of half-god and half-man making for a complete global agenda. Giant step by half-god of half-man, connived with world isms is seems making the total darkness complete. As pro-imperialist man can invent as such, how can we prevent people from thinking that the name of "God" is just the name of the bloody game?

There was recognition that occupation of the Philippines of 1902 was done by mistake and unjust as admitted by McKinley "had come to have doubts" and Roosevelt "recognized the US had make a mistake"[157] but "Protestant missionary press was astonishingly supportive of the brutal war"[158] Seems "god maker" is one giant trapper, justifying the unjustifiable. We began to asking "who is really the god here?"

The Church like IFI saw the greatness of this big God, the Creator of all mankind, the God of whole creation, truth, total and complete. The God that "so loved the world," the greatness of His totality affects and celebrated historically. Man is incapable of limiting Him into half. Omnipresent God is total greatness and total goodness, seen by total man in total situation/reality, seeing it with total capacity. The omnipotent, omnipresent, and omniscience God is the celebration for our salvation (from here and now devilish darkness). Using the name "god" making it "divine" the actions done ungodly who hijacked Him and Christianity, only to know that what they said is a big lie. The big God cannot be contained by creating. In its lonely journey 1902 Filipino-IFI says "we fix our spirit and mind on this God," a truly greater than the weapon of mass destruction. Surely the Lord of justice will be totally revealed one day, as He really is.

Taxpayer Fundamentalist-Christians

Fundamentalist's fundamental thoughts won't care about what kind of military actions should be adopted or should not be applied; won't care about foreign policy with other nations whether it helps them or it hurts them. When they speak with political tone, it must be about the appointed one of "God" to rule the world.' Pushing America to be in the world of "inequality" and the appointed one (USA) must be enthroned. That's the mentality (that does not necessarily represent all American thinking). What kind of Christianity is there when the heart is seems anti-Christ and callous to the reality against life—when Christianity is incapacitating the *love-business* of God (even in political realm) to affect and shape all human lives on earth. They say, "Because we are Christian, we don't mind any political affairs." That's neat, but love-business does not impose boundaries. By implication they say, 'We don't care about life when politics covers it—only when human life is outside political'; again, when is life is outside political?' Can political man not be influenced to be pro people/life and its sustaining Source God? See, we push things of God to be separated from the business of human life only to be trapped as "blesser" of inequality of life when and where the title "appointed" race can only work. But this is why Jesus' mission is to break the walls of exclusivist Jews.

But from the same camp of fundamentalist leaders labeled on religion as "wicked" and another leader from the same—the assassination of one leader who is critical to his political party's foreign interest. We must give justice to God's purpose of life. No one on earth can pretend to see heavenly things only. Of course it's just a game of words in the power of cowardice or product of ignorance with a religious name and claims in it which is obviously not an ism of God. Whether Godliness is something like "on and off" depends on what kind of a person you were talking about or with—or who you wish to please. We made our God one sided, ugly, and irrelevant small (as we misrepresent Him).

We are a *taxpayer;* Christians pay taxes for every item we buy in stores, and are required to submit annual remittances. Therefore we empowered our government which is in real sense, *our,* and these includes military actions. We are empowering agent, indeed, of our foreign interest and policy. Fundamentalist seems say, 'We empower something—we don't care what that action is for, or who will be killed, or what other effects it may have against life? We only care for God, spirit, and heaven for afterlife apart from earth.' No, we should not make these terms of God appear like an enemy and instrument against honesty and truth for life's sake—or words serving as tools of the capitalist. To give justice to God, we should not appear to empower the action that is offensive to the general purpose of God in life.

Taxpaying citizens (and Christians) cannot leave empowering as something we don't care about. We must put a Christian response to it, including the *responsibility* for God and human life. Our prayers must serve the Kingdom of God. People in power are not perfect, but they are subject to temptations. We should offer prayers regarding selfish aggressiveness and for all people a subject of his nervous, panicking power.

Taxpaying (fundamentalist) Christians are also *voters* of the one who may spend the tax money. Voters and taxpayers cannot excuse ourselves by saying, "I have nothing to do with what I enthroned and empowered." Christians won't empower something to be selfish dominant *beast*, do we? Instead, we care because we have purpose in this world. We are to bless human life and the purposes of God in life. Christianity should not be blinded with the "light" for power, forcing miracles, magic, healing, and weaponry. How about the wisdom of Jesus in greatness? It is in service and the first will be last! Is he wrong? We'll see how true it is in the end! We see it in our money—in God we trust. We know that the word is greater than where it is written.

Can We Separate Biblical Truth from the Truth of Life?

I began to reflect when I heard a question: "There is only one Bible—why there are so many Churches?" What's the difference? Men and women,—Christian or claiming to be—use the name of God or used by God as they claimed it, making it appear sacred what they had selfishly or doing real *selfless* actions for the sake of goodness. These contribute to why we have so many Churches believing in one Bible. The question can be offensive and stupid to those who believe that truth of life is not limited to the Bible. Only the man with eyes covered by the literal Bible can see the question above as right.

History must be *counted* to understand the truth of man. If a man did some foul thing, someone will respond with equal opposite reactions. The Civil War was true, George Washington was true; Philippine Encomendero and friar abuse were true, Filipino patriotic reactions were true as well. Yes, the Bible didn't say so, but it doesn't mean it was not true. Some Church leaders are guilty of teaching that the only source of truth is the Bible (which is not the intention of it, but can be used to rebuke the other side of truth). No, human *truth* is also recorded in the history book. Their experience, exercise, hardship, and cries for life are their truth. Imperialism is true—and so is the nationalism.

Truth in humanity is not limited with our religious and spiritual truth, but truth is truth of total man (with heart, mind, spirit and strength). Yes, one Christian group is separated from another because of political, social, and moral issues seen after the *inability* to submit to the wisdom of Christ. As a matter of fact, is separated from Christ except from the name "Christian." No human can pretend that history is nothing—except the bad guys in history. No human is immune to the created darkness—unless you learn to act like a beast. Jesus as the light must be lifted up for this darkness.

Human experience and history determines which Church is detaching the Light (of life, Jesus) from the sustained darkness by greedy spirits. God's designed nature is displayed by those who seek for justice, love, and righteousness. The Bible is not Words directing the minds to heaven and spirits *away* from the facts of darkness making the ruler of the world successful. The Bible should bring God to earth not that it brings mind/focus to heaven. If we know the truth of actions and human reactions, the struggle of nations and race against evils, then the question above is nothing. The idea that *truth is found only* in the Bible is myth. Human experience is the measure of Biblical importance. Evil action ruins, but love sustains life. The truth is in history too. The Bible's claim should be affirmed by it. Indeed, you cannot separate Bible truth from the truth of life. Only the offenders of God's purpose will want to separate them, if not deny them or use them for selfish assertion.

Many 'guilty' pastors makes people think that Christianity's Gospel is *irrelevant*—or that Jesus has nothing to do with our life here and now (denying His claim as the *light* of the world). But what is put in action that violates people's right to exist is dictated by his belief, philosophy, or reasons in the heart, mind, spirit, and strength in which Jesus said to be *filled* with our love for God. He said, "Love the Lord your God with all your heart, mind, spirit and strength." This is not something that commanded us to separate ourselves from the talk of life in this world, but it should affect the world. The Bible is the book of truth about the wisdom of God for life, while history book is for facts of events that make us see that darkness is built if Word *for life* is not.

Is Dogmatism Not for the Pro-Life/People Movement?

Dogmatism or doctrinism is like a wall that is built, causing one to label inequalities against others or covering the eyes with rigid judgmental minds. It is sad that the Church became the home of rigid absolutists that use dogma to justify man's anti-life/people movement to satisfy his selfish appetite. Lovers of themselves actually are contradicting the Bible. Biblical dogmatists turned

Christianity into a prison, apart from its very essence. If we think its primary business is to guard the Bible's letter (and not the honest meaning behind it), it is not separated from the cultic religion and biblical literalism that can miss His message's very point. The Pharisee way is not Jesus' way of looking at the Bible and the Sabbath law.

Selective literal dogmatism is what we got when the end of our Christianity is the Bible, letters, word, and phrases or chapter and verse. This is creating venues of man's thoughts separated from the actual life's situation so that man can play and dance between two entities: "spiritual/religious being" versus "human/social being." In that case, there comes a time that we should push Christian religion away from us because our social being must address our social crisis.

In giving justice to our traditional way of treating the Bible, we need a dogmatic approach in our theology because we need to be strengthened from the confusing literalism held by literal-minded fundamentalist fanatics. But Christianity is not for dogmatism to make it passive insensitive to the demand of actual life/people's situation that threatens life.

Jesus is not callous against sick people, Romans, Gentiles, Samaritan sinners, or women when they needed him. His being Jewish did not make him passive against the racist and exclusivist spirit of the people in power. Christian religion should not serve against life. Jesus is pro-life beyond literal-mindedness—and pro-life beyond preserving his Jewishness. His Christianity is revolutionizing tradition, ritual, literal mindedness, back to loving (for all kind of people beyond racial boundaries), service (for the needy/poor); not judgmental (but embrace and inclusive), brotherhood among those who loved and believed God—not to Biblical dogmatism.

If we start talking about life's cry, struggle, what brings happiness, love, respects, justice and peace, we end up bringing real worship back of humans to God. Humans are capable of recognizing the beauty, appreciating the value, and seeing the real importance of things that belongs to God—if our human nature is not wrapped by religious isms such as dogmatism and rigidity with absolutist close mindedness. God did not expect us to worship Him because we are being deceived or blinded by the "light" of claims or by religious dogmatism. Human beings are situated in the rightful place; it is enough to cause him to worship. In the sanctity of human life, we celebrate God. Peace is between human beings full of life—founded, grounded, and connected in the sources of life the Creator. We may need aid to direct the real worship to Him beyond confusion—but not as instruments against life or people.

Chaotic war is a product of worship of self—to justify the selfish desire that involves lies, claims, deception, injustice, anger, insecurities, and fear. Preserving life brings beauty, appreciation, happiness, and love to all things that are opposite to war anger, intimidation, injustice and racism. It brings worship to the Creator.

Again, history is important and should not be covered by religious dogmatism and racial claims. Honest people asked why man needed to use lies and deception to position for global rule to serve life. Why demonize others to justify the invasion of nations and expect to be worshipped as savior? Great dogma (if we must call it) says, "Love God with all your heart you heart mind, spirit and strength; and love your neighbor as yourself, in which and because there is no other greater than these, and in which hang all the law and the prophet." Where we are is the place where the truths of these must be pointed out to serve life and people, and so, must be celebrated.

Can Religion Stop the Ability to Learn from Historical Experience?

Religion that is detached from the ideals of the past history won't care about people's struggles in the past. It has no interest in bringing in the experiences of the people—no grasp of the relationship between history and what kind of loving community they should base the foundation on. But religion can halt the human ability to embrace the reasons or wisdom of history—and its understanding of the wrong from right. By that, religion can kill the ability to point out the meaning of Christianity in relation to life's endeavor, the role of faith in human historical freedom, to see the light of Jesus for the darkness of imperialism or racism, and the capacity to lift up the glory of God manifested in history after the failures of man's selfish interest and own way that is put as the center stage of life.

If you belong to the class or part of the nation tagged by the label 'inferior race'—just because one race has that notion being superior—you know that this is certainly part of the problem that humans should talk about. This is part of justice and equality issues that all should think and reflect upon, but your race is hit by it. The victim or involved cannot talk about it in order to protect the image of your religion. That is the enemy of the core message of Christianity. The very purpose of the Church of Christ is defeated right there and the spirit of the dogmatist religion has prevailed.

Religion (of dogma, claims, religious discipline, ritual and fanaticism) is not necessarily the same with Christianity of God's love, righteousness, relationship with others, equality, brotherhood, justice, and respect to human dignity. Religion (as not sympathetic to freedom-history) can kill your normal understanding of things in exchange for religious naiveté. This can keep you away from being critical in a very critical condition. Religion can make you opposite to Jesus' expectation to celebrate freedom. God's Kingdom should be celebrated in human life. This is why nationalistic Church of historic people is rich with the lessons of history. After almost four hundred years of slavery of Filipinos by foreign rules, Filipinos are now supposedly rich in experience, lesson, and philosophy. Sadly, the Romanist religion seems nailed the Filipino mind to be naïve and bound in colonial mentality. It seems to be the same with the purpose and enthusiasm of late nineteenth century Fundamentalists (as the idea of imperialism began to take force). Surely, history keeps repeating because the interest to know and learn the lesson or wisdom is faded—and religion contributed much of the killing of the *ability* to reflect theologically the role of history in building up life of community and the capacity to grow mature from historical experiences. Religion must be saved from the motive of imperialism—to have power for national salvation and to give life in human relationship beyond colors.

In Dualism, Does God Seem Captivated by the Bible-Ism?

The dualistic system is asserted to be God's way of dealing the truth. Is it what really God is? Or are you creating that kind of God's nature and character so that one's fanatic/racist and selfish interest can play around with it and a dualistic "God" can take one side only and may serve the capitalist agenda? Oh no! So much of God makers here! We know now who can kill "God." We know those who are not comfortable with the idea of free, loving God. Dogmatists and absolutists of this world for Biblically imprisoned "God" may shout in your face about their religious piece. Some claimed as "teachers" were confident about their "truth" (even though wrongs) in front of anybody's faces: 'The Bible said, "God is, therefore you must."' Wrong confidence is dangerous, but the God of love is like Jesus acting on religious Sabbath, favoring the helpless, weak, and sick. Biblical Sabbath law cannot imprison Jesus to do good things to those in need—against the absolutism of hypocritical religious claimants. Life-centered Christianity is of love/life-centered God.

Our care for human life determines whether we have to believe in that "God" of book and doctrine or not. In fact, we don't have to believe in God if that God is racist and puts weak (or colored) people in line behind the unjust superiors. I say many thanks to my loving and merciful God of justice for showing us the other way—the truth of Him. He is not an imprisoned God of book, but is a free God of life that causes anyone normal and complete human to worship Him and free them. He is for human's freedom and equal treatment before He is judge of the end time (against the sinners) like in Prodigal son story. He is for life and healing the sinners before He is for the Biblical absolutism. He is for love and mercy before He is for perfect religiosity, according to the expectations of Temple leaders. He is for service and self's emptiness before man's greatness. He is for life before he is for the spirit to go to heaven after death. For the total man with heart, mind, and soul, God is "worshipable." For users/manipulator of God, He must be confined in the pages of the Bible—a God of doctrine, chapter, and verse.

The *spirit-only* man must remain spiritual only (incapable of seeing the total events of life), incapable of feeling the reality of ruining deception/lies against human's national and cultural order; incapable of recognizing the evil things done to human life in history. He is incapable of seeing the reality before he can worship God and feel good in hypnotizing heaven and religious spiritualism. Why deprive God of His design of us? We are created as total man and complete— no matter how this nature makes the imperialist and capitalist man uncomfortable. Love God with all your totality: heart, mind, soul, spirit, and strength. Love is not spirit business. "Love your neighbor as yourself" is not about spiritual thing either; it is about life's relational, social-human being on earth. In *The God Makers,* Ed Decker tells us that there is such thing as "god maker." To reflect on it, this god is small "g" meaning not the one we believed in, is worshiped by "god-makers" entrepreneur believer of new things with the spirit of anti-tradition, anti-institution or anti-mainstream, anti-historical when it comes to religion or Church. But these 'makers' at the same time are believer of institutions which has the power to maneuver of ruling the world and acquiring territorial expansion.

The concept of the 'blessing of God' based on half-man's ability to make/create according to his limited thinking (false image), changed the meaning of the word "blessing" and the function of things relative to the character of the created god. "Blessing" in this case, is based on man's ability to consume the capitalist/entrepreneur's material product in the world of capitalist/globalist market. Of course, in that thinking, yesterday's sign of richness is today's symbol of being poor as things become obsolete. Tomorrow's shame with behind kinds of materials, property, or obsolete technology/materials can be the same. Indeed, "blessing" is according to his idea (and the god that he thought should say "Amen" to him!). What a different from the concept of Christ's teaching of humility!

Someone asked, "What do you mean, stay poor because we are Christian?" God did not create half-man's concept of "blessing" in which the actuality of that "blessing" goes to big corporation marketers first—and people are trapped investing all their time and energy to catch up paying the debts in the flow of the world's standard that consumerism put into. Man-made god is a blesser of the agenda of the fittest winners. What a world of lies that god-makers is making. In this case, it is not God at all that is worshipped, but the god-maker is served by a god as his thought product. Agents of darkness in the end will be identified. The Lord of truth will be glorified.

VII
Religions of Self and End Time

The **Word of Faith Movement** is another Christian movement of cultic (sect or non denominational religion) in America. It is the product of early twentieth century mental shaping. The movement centers on health, wealth, and prosperity gospel. People of this type of Christianity are fed and sustained to be in touch with the teachings (of the "teachers") on television networks. The teachings are in the living room of every Americans and the people of the world because of the support of people sold out to their focus teaching. People gave money with the hope that they could get a hundredfold back as promised. It's about self and a mental attitude for prosperity.

Look back to the founders of the movements. Though Kenneth Erwin Hagin was termed "Father of the Faith Movement," the man who deserved to be called father of this was Essek W. Kenyon. He developed the idea that Hagin is copying. "Many of the phrases teaching popularized by today's prosperity teachers, such as 'What I confess, I possess,' (or if I say I can have the car, I can have it because I said it) came originally from Kenyon."[159] Kenyon earned his knowledge mainly from Emerson College of Oratory. He learned about *New Thought* ideas, a system of cultic belief taught that true reality is spiritual—and that the spiritual is the cause of all physical effects. The human mind—through positive mental attitude and positive confessions—has the power to create its reality: either health and wealth, or sickness and poverty.[160]

Frederick K. C. Price claimed to be influenced by Kenneth Hagin. Charles Capps claimed that most of his teaching came from Hagin. John Osteen of Lakewood Outreach Center claimed that Hagin was his introduction to the Faith Movement. Kenneth Copland—as of 1988—was the *ex officio* leader of the Faith Movement. He said, "When Hagin speaks, he still listens." Why did Kenyon get into this? McConnel revealed that Kenyon said, "We cannot ignore the amazing growth of Christian Science, Unity, New Thought and Spiritism. The people who are flocking to them are not the ignorant masses, but the most cultured and wealthy of the land, and their strongest appeal is the supernatural elements of their so called religions—the testimonies of healing are their strongest asset."

In his attempt to respond to the cults and offer a Christian alternative to their beliefs and practices, Kenyon incorporated metaphysical cults into his theology. As a result, his syncretism of cultic ideas—in which the sad truth is that the cultic, not the biblical, element of the Faith theology—are the very elements that distinguish it the most. They occupied center stage. It contradicted to phrases and teachings of the Bible that do not condemn the poor, humble, and the sinners (Lk 6:20; 4:18; Mk 10:21, 14:7, 6:24; Mk 10:25; Mt 6:19–21; 6:24; Mk 12:44; Gal. 2:10; 1 Cor. 11:22; Mk 4:19; 1 Tim. 6:17, 18,19; Jas 2:5; 5:1–3).

See what we can get if we center ourselves to number? Say what people like to hear for self-centered reward! It is not about social justice, identifying evils in man's actions, or brotherhood of all; it is about *self*. Like this seems to be the reasons why Church is described as "opium" of the society, denying the actual reality by man-made forces of evils that violated the nations' sovereignty and independence. "God became the *means* thereby the end of prosperity is attained."[161] Truly, "name it and claim it" gospel is like submission to the temptations of Satan to Jesus seems to be like "don't do your next plan to serve people but satisfy yourself with personal power and abundance with material things and prestige, (see Mt 4:1–8; Lk 4:1–13).

Manfred Brauch wrote:

It is probable that no other issue affect the lives of Christians more directly than that of health and wealth and their relationship to the will of God. Is it God's intention that believers experience good physical health? Is it a Christian promised financial success by virtue of his or her faith in Christ? If a Christian does not experience these blessings, is he or she outside the will of God? This is dependent on how one interprets the Bible … *Time* magazine devoted a cover story on "Prosperity Gospel" movement. Also known by such names as the "Health and Wealth Gospel" and "Name It and Claim It," its proponents include Christian authors, mega church leaders, and TV personalities such as Joel Osteen, Kenneth Hagin, T. D. Jakes, Benny Hinn, and Kenneth Copeland … Essential aspects of their understanding of biblical teaching may be summarized in this pronouncement: "You can have what you say." "We can write our own ticket with God if we decide what we want, believe that it's ours, and confess it." "He wants you rich and healthy." "What is the desire of your heart? Name it, claim it by faith, and it's yours! The heavenly Father has promised it. It's right there in the Bible." The claim that this message is biblical has been subject to strong criticism. Some have said that it rests, at best, on a simplistic theology and leads to misguided ways of living, and at worst, it is dangerous. Historical theologian Michael Horton of Westminster Theological Seminary states that it is based on "a twisted interpretation of the Bible" and is "a wild and wacky theology." Noted New Testament scholar Gordon Fee speaks of it as a diseased understanding of biblical truth. Has this health-and-wealth gospel emerged because of the abuse of selectivity, and is it, therefore, "a different gospel" in contrast to the authentic gospel (Gal 1:6–7)?[162]

Deification Teaching

Deification teachers are teaching "deification" of man (meaning "man is little god" or "man is god"). Deification teachers (or little god-teachers mostly being watched on the TV are supported by desperate individuals) saying that 'man is god.' Teachers are coming from the same religion mentioned above. Of course, these will contradict to the concept in the Bible regarding self-emptying and cross-bearing Christianity. In *The Agony of Deceit* (edited by Michael Horton), we read the thoughts of R. C. Sproul that must be known to all. "We know in history books about the heretical teaching 'Apotheosis' (becoming God). Many of the 'modern Gnostics' (or revival of Gnosticism) claim to know many things that others didn't know." Because Church (or ecclesiastical) history is not taken seriously, repetition of the mistakes is inevitable.[163]

The teaching of deification is tempting to people to drop the orthodoxy of Christian teachings and embrace the self-centered teachings. It is very attractive to people who are not critical and cannot see the danger. This makes Christianity "for personal interest" and absolutely supportive to the self-centeredness of the weak or to those who wanted to act as God, hypnotizing the vulnerable subjects away from the liberating teaching of the historical nationalistic Christianity. Here, for our awareness, we simply look at some lines of simplistic teachings from "little god" teachers: Essek W. Kenyon said, "The Lord Jesus was not, however, a 'one-of-a-kind.' 'Incarnation' can be repeated in each and every one of us. Every man who has been 'born again' is an Incarnation."[164] Repeating the idea Kenneth Copeland said, "Every man who has been born again is an incarnation and Christianity is a miracle. The believer is as much an incarnation as was Jesus of Nazareth … God has been reproduced on the inside of you."[165] Copeland also said, "You need to realize that you are not a spiritual schizophrenic—half-God and half-Satan—you are all God. The problem area is not in your spirit; it lies in your mind and body"[166] He said, "You don't have God in you. You are one." [167]

Kenneth Hagin said, "Jesus was first divine, and then he was human. So he was in the flesh a divine-human being. I was first human, and so were you, but I was born of God, and so were you, but I was born of God, and so I became a human-divine being!" He looked at himself as "God-Man."[168] He said, "You are as much the incarnation of God as Jesus Christ was. Every man who has been born again is an incarnation and Christianity is a miracle. The believer is as much an incarnation as was Jesus of Nazareth." [169]

Earl Paulk said, "Adam and Eve were placed in the world as the seed and the expression of God. Just as dogs have puppies and cats have kittens, so God has little gods … We have trouble comprehending this truth … until we comprehend that we are little gods, and we begin to act like little gods, we cannot manifest the Kingdom of God." [170]

Paul Crouch of Trinity Broadcasting Network (TBN) said, "I am little god. I have His name. I am one with Him. I'm in covenant relation. I am a little god. Critics be gone."[171]

Robert Tilton said, "You are … a God kind of creature. Originally you were designed to be a god in this world. Man was designed or created by God to be the god of this world …"[172]

Casey Treat said, "Oh, I don't know about you, but that does turn my crank! An exact duplicate of God! Say it out loud—I'm an exact duplicate of God!" [173]

In interview by Paul Crouch of TBN, Fred Price said, "All right, we're the children of God. We've been recreated and have been made new creatures in Christ Jesus. So I'm God as much as your sons are Crouches (interviewer). But certainly I'm not God God, the Creator God …"[174]

Very detached from human history, they felt freely without criteria from historical sense. They teach whatever individuals of imperialist country want to hear. But in honest worship to God we must be reminded that Eve was tempted by Satan to rebel against God, saying, "You will be like God" (Genesis 3:5).

Self-Centered in Latter Day God

Recently out of the Latter Day Saints (LDS) or Mormonism, a gay fellow spoke on NPR radio. He was not happy because he had been told to marry a woman to wipe out his gayness. He would be promoted (as all Mormons are) to the status of being "god." Being gay, the chance of becoming god is out. Therefore he must not be—even though he actually is—gay. He said further that there were wives and children out there who were left behind by their gay husbands and gay fathers after realizing that husband or father was actually a gay. Women and children became victims of the "wiping out of gayness" solution that didn't work. (The solution was based on the thinking that being gay is a sin).

Ed Decker was a Latter Day Saint (LDS) for twenty years—a member of the Melchizedek Priesthood—but he left LDS in 1976, and wrote a book about Mormonism; He stated, "In Mormon thought, angels are on a kind of spiritual continuum between manhood and godhood. Upon their deaths, certain righteous men become angels. Later, presumably, they become gods. Mormons like to say that a man or woman is a "baby god" or god in-embryo; an angel is an adolescent god; and an "adult god" is a full-fledged deity like the LDS god, Elohim."[175] Mormon President Kimbal has emphasized that "no one becomes a god without a special Temple marriage for eternity." Dr. Harold Goodman, LDS Mission President in England, said, "With our intellect and with our discipline … we can continually grow and develop and become a god …"[176]

How to be saved? The Mormons answer, "Resurrected by grace, but saved (exalted to godhood) by works." What happens after death? The Mormons answer, "Eventually nearly everyone goes to one of three separate heavenly 'kingdoms,' with some achieving godhood."[177] Again deification teaching is like submitting to the temptation of Satan to Eve to rebel against God to be "like God."

It is sad to think that people are taught to be self-centered in their regard of Christianity contradicting all teachings about cross-bearing sacrifices for the sake of Christ's purpose for other people, or contradicting all self-emptying and humility teachings for serving others. Instead, it can allow the sin of inhospitable people like those of Sodom (Gen. 19:4–8, or Lev. 19:18). Loving your neighbors can be ignored by people fixated to the self reward to be god and in heaven.[178] This can cause ignoring the devastation and violence to people after invaders' assertion.

End Time Religion: Fundamentalist, Millennial/Dispensationalist, and Born-Againism

One friendly pastor invited me to attend a "revival" meeting. At that fellowship meeting, I saw jumping, crying, and displays of emotion (which is not a problem for me). It caused me though to ask God to show me clearly why I was not totally convinced that Christianity has to be like that (thinking that what I saw represents the trend of emotionalism). What I witnessed became my affirmation to what I already thought regarding Millennialists, Dispensationalists, and Fundamentalists as they start from *end time* doctrines and beliefs by saying that the Second Coming and End of the World must not be neglected and should be taken seriously as the most important teaching. (I hear a lot of that in 1980s since my boyhood from the aggressive fundamentalist preachers in local village). Being fearful, alert, and watchful is one conditioning of a character. To sustain and follow up that in mind, they teach end time Bible literalism. Since it was alerted to the congregants, they expected to hear the same themes whole their lives for all their heart, mind, emotion, and focus, which to them is the "good preaching."

To keep the attention and alertness pointed to high heaven, it must be said always that the Christ's Second Coming is *imminent*! Every war and calamity is counted as a sign of the truth. They say, 'Stay strong in their Church for sure salvation to heaven.' The members were fearful, but excited about the promises of personal reward such as assurance of their self-reward in rapture. They didn't have the capacity to ask who did what in the unjust war, who made nuclear weapons, who build the culture of war; instead they view them as sign and instrument for the fulfillment of the end time prophecy.

This became their ultimate way of converting people from historically grounded Christianity, mainstream Catholicism, and Protestantism. This seems to be an effective way of *derailing* the interest from the core (Kingdom of God) to the *fringes*—from a message of life to the end time, from Kingdom of God to mental capturing speculations. Now because end time speculations included thoughts that Satan wants to rule the world—in their world view— there are only two realities: God and Satan, and that the world is of Satan and God is in heaven. This is powerful enough to steal the attention from advancing the "Kingdom of God and His will" to be done on earth, to be thinking of relocation to heaven.

Disgraceful as it seems to be, while 'end time' is waited, 'end time' people lift up America as "called by God to be the defender of Christian ideals in an unchristian world, or join an ideological crusade against godless Communism."[179] When it ruins, destroys, invades, violates, employs falsehood, deception or lies, they seems don't want to know, Fundamentalist-millennial-dispensationalist people sang the chorus as what they wish to be, "God Bless America" —identifying God in action of war against other humans (must not be blessed). However many ruinous mistakes there may be—it is justifiable in their eyes! Not only that, it creates a culture of anger, insecurities and uncertainty they were pinning the name of God in murderous actions. Beating the drums of illegal action naturally caused a bad name for Christianity.

Deception, lies, falsehood, and tricks were employed in 1898 to Emilio Aguinaldo regarding his long desired freedom of the Philippines. It has been used to change the mind of many in the US Congress for the ratification of the 1898 Treaty of Paris, resulting bloodshed of war and the death of many innocent Filipinos. Fundamentalists seemed unable to get that and purposely avoided knowing it. The Iraq War issue is covered in books, including thousands of mentions of lies, deceptions, falsehood, but Fundamentalists cannot get that. It is "none of our business" (as political) when it comes to others, but it is definitely God's issue when it comes to America. What does that bloody devilish represents? Is it about God who loved the world? Or the one who wanted to rule and own the world? Of course, people of the world cannot be fooled—even the rock group Scorpions sang "We don't own the world."

Yes, the Bible predicted that the end would come, but Jesus said, "No one should know." We must continue doing what is good to people and life—otherwise, all will be obsessed and fixated about the Second Coming while blind to what can cause the exploitation of earth. Yes, there is a prediction, but our Godly call is still to serve the creation, people, and life—not covering the world exploitation for *self.* We should not exploit, destroy, or manipulate the earth because as it said "anyway it is just our temporary home."

President Ronald Reagan's secretary of the interior James Watt, a member of the Assembly of God denomination, took Dispensationalism (a systematized look at the Bible as God-working by every thousand years to end time) even further, from neglect of the natural world to outright exploitation. Watt said, "We will mine more, drill more. Cut more timber."[180] (No wonder a lot of people who don't have the means to exploit are living so far behind miserably). On February 5, 1981, Watt suggested that he was not overly concerned about preserving the environment because the imminent Second Coming of Jesus ultimately would render such all efforts irrelevant."[181] In that case, instead of thinking fundamentalist or Pentecostalist or Assembly of God, etc., we should maybe rather adopt the thinking of John Dominic Crossan who wrote, "The second coming of Christ is what will happen when we Christians finally accept that the first coming was the only coming and start to cooperate with its divine presence."

This seems to lead to more "already-presence of God's Kingdom as the Great Divine Cleanup of the world" rather than to "own, exploit, then leave" mentality. We may do all we can to preserve the only earth and treat this as if our only home; With that, with all the capacity that we have, we must promote love, righteousness, and respect to all creatures and all humankind as our ally to preserve peace and harmony in the world. In that thought we surely value love, peace, fairness, respect, righteousness, and justice for all people of the world; even in all our hearts, with all our mind and strength, we have the capacity to do them, and we must. We can love God and our fellow man honestly and purely; to obey them here and now can be done—as if there is no other place to go to see them celebrated, experienced, or enjoyed. We behave as if these commandments are final, bringing Christ's presence as a Second Coming. In this thinking, don't worry, Christians! This still cannot change the mind of God about our rapture to heaven—He will still do it. This reminds us that "the righteous" in the Bible didn't expect their eternal life (Mathew 25:37). You see, we give things to God that we do not control. Since we should give ourselves to God for whatever He'll do with it, do you really care?

Millennial/Fundamentalist/Dispensational people believed that there is a second home for each person, (the self-centered appeared even in going to heaven) and that, in so doing, they should not appear to be worshiping (or serving and wishing) the "omnipotent, omnipresent" United States—as Fundamentalists wanted to see and pushed it to be. Instead, to please God alone and they should not be afraid to trust and actualize what Jesus said. "He who believes in me will live, even though he dies" (Jn 11:25). Then, we must offer ourselves to establish justice, to make peace in this world, serve the purpose of God, and to make His will be done on earth.

It seems confusing and appeared to be just playing to believe that what matters is heaven, spirit or to be saved from the lake of fire; and then acting as to push and justify America to be more of a superpower? Why must they have omnipotent power (of USA) and the ability to wipe out evils and those who are not likable to them if what matters is heaven and spirit? Truly it is confusing if not about bloody mocker's work.

The situation and crisis in the world was one surely by imperialistic games. If true to their millennial mentality, situations like Communism versus terrorism, etc. should be one opportunity for them to prove the truth of their confession about their type of end time Christianity. Why not just let the "truth" prove itself by saying prediction is true and that's it? We cannot alter it? Events should be allowed to reveal the millennialist's points; if the Bible said "God will destroy the world," so be it according to the scripture, so to allow the truth of the Bible seen fulfilled (as they thought). But in actuality, what seems to have happened is that man's greedy spirit ruins the world (with hijacked Christianity to make it look good).

What can make our teeth gnash though is that they wanted to see that America has an enemy. The "Left Behind" fiction series is actually pushing Americans to think that they have an enemy who is the representative of Satan. They sell the notion of war for today's United Europe as anti-Christ the 666. Always looking for an enemy and the title "Agent of God" (America) must be justified. Not all Americans think that way, but the cultic mind of the fundamentalist seems absolute to them.

They celebrate to see war between good and evil—in which they were the good—to sustain the dualistic mind they invented. As the millennialists celebrated it, they kept having fellowship for revival for end time enthusiasm for the Second Coming that had failed many times before, but now must be the time (as they wish). On the contrary, the way they positioned themselves seems that this is the only world (to them). America is the instrument of God to protect. So confusing—if not one bloody game in religious terms! But if this religious ism is just part of the game, positioning the innocent naïve heavenward religious as its ultimate player for power? This seems to be what is being revealed in history.

Hypnotizing claims to predict powerful events—enough to make people regard it as the very teaching of Jesus. Some have established congregations because of it. My readings add some facts of failed end time speculations. Benjamin Keach, the seventeenth-century Baptist, predicted that the world will end in 1689. William Miller the founder of the Millerite Movement predicted that the Second Coming would happen on March 21, 1843. Ellen White, founder of the Seventh Day Adventists (SDA), gave many predictions on years around 1850; all failed. On June 27, 1850, she said, "Few months from now, as angels said 'the end is coming, prepare, prepare, prepare.'" Joseph Smith, the founder of Mormonism, predicted that Jesus would come in 1891 in one of the leader's meeting. He said, "We have this meeting because God asked this … in fifty-six years (meaning, before 1891). The Jehovah's Witnesses Watchtower Bible and Tract Society stated that, in 1914, the War of Armageddon would begin. The prediction was based on Daniel 4. After 1914, they changed it. They said, "This year, Jesus is leading without being noticed." Harold Camping says May 21, 2011 was 'invisible judgment day,' and the world will end October 21, 2011. Now, why do that to Christ? For many, the method is adopted by sustaining the end time focusing on the closing of the minds of the naïves—and making them fanatically supportive to the cultism of end time. Indeed, fanatics cannot be part of the crusade or ministry to stop the exploiter's exploitation. I hope that the end time enthusiasts will stop wishing for the end of the world and do their part to alter the course that is offensive to life of all people. We should *end* the selfish greediness that can ruin the world. Jesus taught that many who will claim "prophet" with power, performed many miracles in the name of Jesus to be called "evildoers" (Matt. 7:22).

In God's complete freedom, "rapture" seems to be His justice to whom it is due, we don't have to subject it to ridicule, or use it to scare people to convert members, or abuse it to "racket" activities (as some called it. In Kevin Phillip's *American Theocracy*; pp.66, 219, 253).

Selective Biblical Literalists Can Be Oppressive

Literalism is not the purpose of the authors of the Bible—even though parts of the Bible can make sense only if you take them literally. But generally, biblical messages can be missed by absolute literalism in abusing the scripture. They can stop being literal if they want to in many areas. It (selectively) depends on who they want to please and what omnipotent agenda they wanted to serve and be part of. Many examples live in selfish exploitative situations: husbands abuse their wives by quoting the scripture. "Wife, submit to your husband." By taking that literally, selfish exploitation is served. Many negative things followed, relationships are ruined, and heartbreaking situation sets in.

The same is true with those in selfish religious motives playing in influencing ambition. The general message of God is ruined because they use it to serve the *self* of one particular race, one particular claim, or one particular global economic desire. Imagine Fundamentalists aiming to influence the instrument where imperialism should succeed—they could influence the American way of thinking in their control of the world (or the way Americans should use the Christian thoughts in building up the empire). Literalism here can be one game. Then those with cultural achievements of the ancients seen in traditional and mainstream Protestants or nationalistic Churches will be subject to Fundamentalist intimidation using literalism as they wish to label things *pagan*. Then they want the government to allow them to collect money to combat the "un-Christian." Then they want the government to prohibit the precious traditions as a way of saying "they must be wrong in order for me to be right" and say "Christian only" and that means not "Catholic." There is so much work in confusing people in the kingdom of deception, wasted work in the world of dumbness. Traditions from the early Church are to be subjected to their oppression and ridicule. They aimed to have center stage in world imperialism, but they only put the name of God upon the powerful of the world they tend to worship (an idolatrous act). They center what they thought right to intimidate the pro-justice and pro-life/people actions of the mainstream Churches, nationalistic product of human's freedom history.

The definition of idolatry as fundamentalists asserted is seen in the presence of icons and images. If you throw them, you are throwing the sin of idolatry away. An image speaks a thousand words about Jesus and the works of God—especially during the time when the printing press was not invented yet. They do not appreciate what our civilization has achieved because they wanted to say "We know what is right and not them! They must be wrong for me to be right!" They focus on the kingdom away from earth instead the kingdom on earth as it is done in heaven.

The What and When of the Fundamentalist Connection

What is fundamentalism? We've been talking about Christian fundamentalism, but it is good to know what their thinking is when they started the movement. I would say up front that this was created as one product of the mental attitude of Americans during the late nineteenth century. At the same time, the pro-Laissez-faire religious enthusiasts and the businessmen were looking outward for market and raw material were overpowering. The turn of the century was a test of how they thought about their Christian religion, handling their desire, and how they saw other people. This became a hundred years of glory—as pointed out by racial Anglo-Saxon doctrine (of inequality). It also started a hundred years of tribulation as the kingdom of inequality began to be asserted in the Philippines.

Thomas Oden said, "I do not want to offend my evangelical or neo-evangelical colleagues by cheaply and inaccurately pinning the older label 'fundamentalism' on those who long ago disavowed it." He told a story about American Christian Fundamentalists. At a Bible Conference at Niagara in 1895, one thing that these Protestants (turned fundamentalist) did was the "selection of doctrines as a nucleus for Christian thoughts: Plenary inspiration of inerrant scripture, the Virgin birth, the substitutionary theory of atonement, the bodily resurrection of Jesus, and imminent second coming of Christ." Why was this so important when so little notice had been taken of it previously? Because the nineteenth century witnessed the powerful emergence of historical consciousness (Hegel, Darwin, Marx, Nietzsche, Spencer, and so on) that expressed a consuming interest in historical origins and evidence. Despite its protests, fundamentalism was inadvertently swept away by this modern historical consciousness and unwittingly became an instrument of it."[182] George Eldon Ladd wrote, "The fundamentalists ... argued that one must take his start from the biblical message, at the heart of which stood such fundamentals of the faith as the Virgin birth, the deity of Christ, the reality of His miracles, His vicarious death, His bodily resurrection, His second coming, and the plenary inspiration of the Scriptures."[183]

Allan J. Lichman wrote, "Despite deep historical roots, fundamentalism emerged as a self-conscious movement when British and American theologians, financed by California oil magnate Lyman Stewart and his brother Milton, published and widely circulated *The Fundamentals: A Testimony to the Truth,* twelve volumes of conservative theological writings dating from 1910 to 1915."[184]

Eric W. Gritsch showed us the more detailed of the development and the *connections* of the Fundametalist, Millenialist, and Dispensationalist (which the generic name is Fundamentalist). The drive to unite the Anglo-America Protestants through agreement on fundamental truths reached its peak with the publication of *The*

Fundamentals. Published with the "compliments of two Christian laymen," the periodicals had eleven editions. Three million copies were sent free of charge to "English-speaking Protestant pastors, evangelists, missionaries, theological students, Y.M.C.A. secretaries, Y.W.C.A. secretaries, Sunday School superintendents, religious lay workers, and editors of religious publications throughout the earth."[185]

Lyman and Milton Stewart, natives of Pennsylvania, had made a fortune in oil. Both were chief stockholders in the Union Oil Company in Los Angeles and Chicago, and Lyman was company president. A member of Immanuel Presbytarian Church in Los Angeles, Lyman became a Darbyite millennialist, supporting the cause that alerted the world to Christ's Second Coming and propagate biblical literalism and millennialism. Both Lyman and Milton Stewart lamented the growing laxity in matters of faith and morals among Presbyterians. Milton turned his attention to the missionary enterprise, especially in China; Lyman Stewart supported educational institutions committed to Bible study, such as Occidental College and the Bible Institute in Los Angeles. Finally, Lyman became the enthusiastic supporter of a plan to commit the English-speaking Protestant world to a unique effort of evangelization by the publication of *The Fundamentals: A Testimony to the Truth.* The idea for the enterprise appears to have originated with Amzi Clarence Dixon, the millennialist preacher at the Moody Church in Chicago.[186]

Lyman met Dixon in 1909 and Dixon gave him $300,000 toward the gigantic literary undertaking. Milton Stewart also gave his financial backing to the venture. Dixon then established an editorial committee consisting of three clergy and three lay members—all of whom had millennial leanings. Sixty-four authors were chosen to write articles for the periodical—most of them were British and American millennialist veterans. Of the ninety articles that appeared, twenty-nine defended biblical literalism, thirty-one argued the fundamental doctrines of the Princeton theology and the five points of the 1910 General Presbyterian Assembly, and the rest were personal testimonies, attacks on science, and proposals for missions.[187]

The movement called "fundamentalist" found its basis in *The Fundamentals*. Lyman Stewart's Testimony Publishing Company received 200,000 letters praising the movement he had helped to launch. Fundamentalists supported the Scofield Reference Bible, became linked with the American Bible League in 1903, and taught a premillennial dispensationalism. The inspiration of the Bible and speculation about Christ's Second Coming dominated the movement before World War I. Biblical literalism, which had been the steady companion of millennial hopes, was the center of fundamentalism. The five articles in *The Fundamentals* on the inspiration of the Bible are based on the Princeton theology of Warfield and Hodge."[188]

VIII
A Perspective for the Church with Historical Sense

The Kingdom of God: Keeping the Core Teaching

Some people have no idea how it feels to be treated as *nothing* (like Israelites in Egypt, or Filipinos under Spanish/Vatican/American rule) by people who think they are superior. They come to you, grab their Bible, and then offer you their dogma or doctrine. They say, "This is the truth." Quoting verses successfully made some think desperately of going to heaven. They became obsessed and fixated about heaven, not eating pork, being in the book of life, flying at the rapture time, being saved from the lake of fire, and being in the right side when the second coming happens. Jesus said, "I must preach the Kingdom of God … for this is the reason why I was sent" (Lk 4:43). You cannot alter this with scary news about hell.

Jesus was in the Synagogue reading the prophesy of Isaiah about good news to the poor, freedom for the prisoners, and releasing the oppressed. Then Jesus proclaimed, "Today this scripture is fulfilled" (Lk 4:18–20). We should regard this declaration as important. Jesus spent much time preaching the good news of the Kingdom to cities and synagogues with parables. We should spend time preaching the same. It is not giving justice to the Bible if you claim you know— only to divert from the real priority of Jesus.

Some pastors repent because of old piety. Pat Robertson was one of the most watched in TV, influencing the minds of Americans and Filipinos. He is one "teacher" that realized he was wrong to put so much time teaching other themes besides the Kingdom of God. He stated, "This was revolutionary understanding, as simple as it may seem these six or seven years later. I had been instructed to regard our time as the age of the church, and it is that in a very real sense; but John the Baptist and later the Lord Jesus Christ declared the arrival of the Kingdom of God. Somehow I had failed to take seriously the fact that the Kingdom of God is the central teaching of Jesus."[189] We don't know if his realized wrong was heard by the people and changed their views on the fundamental teaching for honesty's sake.

Author Peter Wagner said, "It is clear to me now that the Kingdom of God is present as well as future that I wonder how I missed it so long ... I finally realized how ignorant of the subject I was ... I now believe that the Kingdom of God should be much more central to our preaching." [190]

Charles "Chuck" Swindoll is one of America's favorite radio preachers. He said that he kept many of his sermons in a file, from there, he looked at the file on the subject of the Kingdom of God, 'embarrassing to say, it is empty, how did I miss it. Central to the whole purpose is Kingdom of God.'[191]

Right Reverend Peter Hall said, "We also hold very dear, as evangelicals, the doctrine of the Second Coming of Christ … Christians having always been taught to welcome the Second Coming, nuclear war then is a thing not to be worried about, but even to be positively welcomed … That attitude is a total distortion of what we are told by Jesus obedience in the light of the Second Coming."[192]

Before this time, what were they teaching and proclaiming about, in the pulpit, on the radio and TV? What subjects did they dwell on so much? What were they putting heavily on the minds of their listeners? What was not core, but was treated as if it was a core teaching of Jesus? More pastors, ministers, and leaders should ask the same forgiveness for being instrumental in making people believe fanatically about the diverting subjects that defines Fundamentalism. Their honest assessments are not fundamental to Jesus, but the believers of Hegel, Darwin, Marx, Nietzsche, and Herbert Spencer were given reason to ridicule the Christian religion. But this is not what concerns us. What concerns us so much is these *derailing* themes and focuses by those "teachers" before— and now sustained by those who embrace it so dearly—positioned themselves in the most influential venue. On the television program, they taught the end of the world theme—it can make each person fixated and fanatically obsessed about personal salvation of the spirit as if this is what matters in Christianity. They close their minds about the Kingdom of God and that created the wrong notion about Christianity. They really do keep people away from the core teachings of the Kingdom of God—consciously or not.

We must listen to the serious scholars studying the contents of the Bible—before the Bible can be used to contradict the very core of the Gospel. We must rescue the Bible from Fundamentalists.

The Kingdom of God is central in Jesus' mission. George Eldon Ladd said, "(Mt 4:17). This theme of the coming of the Kingdom of God was central in His mission." X. Leon-Dufour said, "The kingdom of God is at hand." This is the principal aim of John the Baptist and Jesus (Mt 3:1; 4:17). A. J. Wilhelm said, "The central theme of Christ preaching is the good news of the Kingdom of God." Henry Blackaby said, "The Kingdom of God was the heart of Jesus's teaching and preaching." Pat Robertson said, "Indeed He described such teaching as His ultimate purpose (Lk 4:43)." John Bright said, "For the concept of the Kingdom of God involves, in a real sense, the total message of the Bible." *The Kingdom of God*, an Abingdon award winner, is "one of the most satisfactory in biblical theology."

The Kingdom of God

We desired to see—and make others see—that our Christian teaching is a blessing, and not imprison people's mind so that the imperialist powerful ruler can be successful and teaching the Bible as a means. No! Honesty is still great to make us all see what is it that makes Jesus's teaching have sense, by directing one's mind to the Kingdom of God theme. Some key words, phrases, and texts from the Bible tell us why this subject is so important. Jesus's disciples were looking for him early in the morning as he went to a solitary place for refreshment and prayer. As they found him, Jesus spoke to them about what he should do next, "I must proclaim the good news of the Kingdom of God ... for I was sent for this purpose" (Lk 4:43). Jesus was in our world for the purpose of proclaiming the Kingdom of God. How dare us not mind it because we make people obsessed about other things?

Jesus began his public ministry in Galilee by saying, "The time is fulfilled, and the Kingdom of God has come near, repent" (Mk 1:14–15). Jesus went about all the cities, teaching in their synagogues about the Kingdom of God (Mt 9:35). One of Jesus's teachings seems to require that we all should put the Kingdom of God first. "Seek first his kingdom and his righteousness" (Mt 6:33). Jesus taught how to pray—not only because his disciples asked them—so believers should know how to pray. Jesus said, "Your kingdom come. Your will be done on earth" (Mt 6:10). Jesus taught that his Father's good pleasure is "to give you the kingdom" (Lk 12:32). Jesus called his disciples to be sent for ministry for the Kingdom of God (Lk 9:1–2). Jesus sent the seventy to proclaim the Kingdom of God. He said, "Say to them 'The Kingdom of God has come near to you'" (Lk 10:8–9). Jesus's parables were His way of teaching his disciples about the Kingdom of God. "To you has been given the secret of the kingdom of God, but for those outside, everything comes in parables" (Mk 4:11). Jesus declared to Pilate that he was born for this (Jn 18:37). The law and the prophets were in effect until John the Baptist came; since then, the good news of the kingdom of God is proclaimed (Lk. 16:16). Jesus spent His forty days after resurrection "appearing to them during forty days and speaking about the kingdom of God" (Acts 1:3).

Here we want to point out that in every strategic event, Jesus teaches and proclaims the Kingdom of God as his core teaching.

Paul regarded the teaching of Jesus well enough for us to know that he spent two years proclaiming the Kingdom of God (Acts 28:30–31). We must rescue the core teaching of the Kingdom of God from people who want to imprison it. Christians must put it in the center of learning of Christian living here and now—instead of centering the departure for heaven.

Jesus established the movement before his Sermon on the Mount, seen in the Gospel of Luke (6:12 ff). Jesus spent the night praying for the great and serious event that would take place the next day. It looked like there was one big event assembly (or convention, to use our term). A large crowd of his disciples were there, great number of people from all over Judea, Jerusalem, from Tyre and Sidon came. That day, he called his disciples whom He prepared for the great purpose; then from this great crowd he chose the twelve to be called Apostles. It looked like He was forming a huge formal religious/spiritual body—with his Apostles as his core "cabinet" members. He declared his agenda— like a state of the nation—in front of the disciples and people. We learned many things about Jesus' conversation with religious leaders, teachers of the law, and individuals; but in the Sermon on the Mount, he taught many things with complete authority.

On this strategic occasion, what was his message? The Beatitudes said, "Blessed are you who are poor, for yours is the kingdom of God." It looks like the business of the Kingdom involves the business for the affected and poor. He declared that Isaiah was talking about Him as the fulfillment of this: "The Spirit of the Lord is on me, because he anointed me to preach good news to the poor" (Lk 4:16; Mt 5). Jesus affirmed himself to John that he was the one who was to come. "The good news is preached to the poor" (Lk 7:18, 22). This is not saying that the poor are favored, but if Church business is to be an agent for the order of life (based on God's purpose), poorness is the symptom of what should be changed! It is understandable to start from the affected poor if the Kingdom of love and righteousness is to be fulfilled for all. Poor people are indicators that something must be done in the system of governance. Here we learn that the business of Jesus' Kingdom is for life and not so much for spirit or heaven. (Heaven does not need so much of formula).

Kingdom of God and the End Time Themes

In God's sovereign reign, He is obeyed. His commandments are followed; The prayer, "Our Father ... hallowed be your name, your kingdom come your will be done on earth as it is in heaven" (Mt 6:9–10) is realized. His name is hollowed, honored, respected, and worshipped. If His will and commandments are done, the national, social and political situations of people shall see God as the source of peace and order.

Being exposed to Fundamentalist fellowship, meetings, radio, and television, I learned to say, "If we want to follow Jesus, we should start from Jesus." Our Bible may say everything that can derail our attention from the very heart of Jesus's proclamation, dependent so much on how we handle the truths in the Bible, the primacy of his teaching—and the core of his preaching—depends on how we treat the Bible. Taking His words seriously—particularly his commandments—is one reflection of our worship of Him. Jesus said, "Heaven and earth will pass away, but my words will never pass away" (Lk 21:33). Law and the prophet points to Jesus (the Word), the giver of the commandments in which "all the Law and the Prophets hang on" (Mt 22:37).

I reflect on Luke 21:25–32 during the Advent season: Fundamentalists are feasting on *end time* themes, such as the Second Coming, the end of the world, the lake of fire, and the rapture—as if such is the very teaching of our Lord. Those themes didn't really change the priorities of Jesus. His Great Commission is still his great commission (Mt 28:18–20). "Seek ye first the Kingdom of God and His righteousness" (Mt 6:33). "The Kingdom is the reason why I was sent" (Lk 4:43). "I was born for it" (see Jn 18:36). These definitive words should be treated the way Jesus said them. Many Fundamentalist congregations were created because of exaggerated interpretations of scary news about endless years in the lake of fire against the Kingdom of God. Through these, many of people were converted from IFI and mainstream churches. They gave predictions and converted our people at the same time. The predictions failed, but they turned the falsified wordings into other interpretations— except the people and big amount of money were not returned.

The Kingdom of God talks about life or its conditions (here and now), while the eschatological/future event themes dwell so much on doctrine and selective Bible and interpretations of chapter and verses in their Bible-ism. In them, the effects of Christianity would be thought or become (as it did) a religion of doctrine and dogma, can get people stuck in books and claims rather than dwelling on the business of life according to God's plan in Christ. They dwell so much on the future's end-time signs rather than involving people in building up the kingdom of God.

The Gospel tells us about "cosmic signs: sun, moon and stars; nations will be in anguish ... men will faint from terror" (Lk 21:25). This signifies that the world "will be in chaotic state, out of control."[193] Jesus continued, "Even so, when you see these things happening, you know that the kingdom of God is near" (Lk 21:31). Christianity is not about dwelling on signs, but living in submission to God's dominion, His rules, and His commandments. What is it that He wants us to do to fulfill God's Kingdom?

I say, "We should start from Jesus!" rather than covering and diverting the attention from the teachings that should be treated (justly) the way Jesus regarded and proclaimed them. We should regard with primary importance the way Jesus intend his themes— and the way he valued them. We should accept them the way that we accepted the doctrine of the Trinity (which may not be clear to us, but He gave the word that we must accept justly and humbly).

To follow the King's rule is our individual indicator of whether we are in the Kingdom or not. To be in the kingdom is to follow His commandments.

One of the teachers of the law ... asked him, "Of all the commandments, which is the most important?" Jesus answered, "The most important one is this: 'Hear, O Israel, the lord our God, the Lord is one. Love the Lord your God with all your heart and with all your soul and with all your mind and with all your strength.' The second is this: 'Love your neighbor as yourself.' There is no other commandment greater than these." (Mk 12: 28–31).

These words should be treated great with reverence. All the law and the prophets hang on these two commandments." (Mt 22:37). This must not be covered by end time themes. Jesus said, "A new command I give you: Love one another. As I have loved you, so you must love one another" (Jn 13:34). Though this *new* one did not say that the others are obsolete, but it didn't say other doctrine is more important.

Paul wrote, "Whatever other commandment there may be, are summed up in this one rule: Love your neighbor as yourself. Love does no harm to its neighbor. Therefore love in the fulfillment of the law" (Rom. 13:9–10). James said, "Religion that God our Father accepts as pure and faultless is this: to look after orphans and widows in their distress and to keep oneself from being polluted by the world" (Jas 1:27).

What we learned is not about Biblical *niceness or nicety* and perfectionism, but what are we as people. It is about how we relate to people. It is about relationship and service to people and life rather than intimidations in Biblical perfectionism, and focusing on derailing biblical text away from "Kingdom/Love" themes of Jesus.

If these are done in our lives now, we are creating, shaping, forming, and building the condition of life in which God is the Lord. If the commandments are followed, it is already the Kingdom of God. When He is lord and master in our home, family, and community, this is the Kingdom condition.

We often hear the phrase "Kingdom of God: *already* and *not yet.*" The way I simplify it is this: "already" because we have Jesus in our heart. We loved him so, we cried out for him to stay in our heart, to fill us with His presence. We recognize our dependence to his truths and principles—and we confess that we are nothing away from his teachings.

The Kingdom of God is not yet here because we are still praying. "Your Kingdom come, your will be done on earth." Every day is another day to pray for new conditions, challenges, and subjects for things to be done (for God's reign and purpose). We are still advancing it for the coming generations. New strategies, approaches and faces of Kingdom's enemy remain until the final Day of Judgment.

Meditating on "cosmic signs" (Lk 21:25), we don't know what can cause them. Are we going to be literal about it or not? We just have to cling to the promises of God about them. However, there are things that we can observe: the man-made chaos, uncertainty, destructions, and our kingdom work must be visible. We create the conditions of life in which God is visibly the Lord (in our conduct). We heard about wars, terrorism, extra-judicial killing, human rights violations, famine, human trafficking, climate change, and evils in history, selfish and lovers of themselves that are not hidden anymore. Ugly things—product of man's doing—are done to the maximum full. Man's way (separated from what God wants) is foolish and leads to death, building darkness.

Man is incapable of doing what is good *away* from God. Greediness is not of God; it brings economic chaos. Worship of power and desire to dominate the world brings insecurities. Materialism and other related isms will lead people to see the glory of God in the end. Isms that led to chaos can cause us all to *realize* the greatness and beauty of His command and purpose in life. We will say that day 'If we only followed Him, things would have been great.'

Christian Thinkers Must Be Consulted

To see the relevance of the Kingdom of God subject to the Christian Church, we may be affirmed by some scholars. From our highly respected Biblical reflections on the Gospel of the Kingdom of God, we must learn that so we can help to bring the importance of Christianity to the victims of selfishness and injustice. Dr. George Eldon Ladd said, "Six of the beatitudes are cast in a futuristic setting" (Mt 5:4–9). The fulfillment of the happiness looks beyond the course of this age to a time when conditions are changed—when grief, aggressiveness, acquisitiveness, sin, and violence no longer dominate human society. Only with the end of the course of this world and the establishment of a new world order can each be transformed into unmixed joy. Throughout this age, power and aggressiveness find a ready reward, but the promise that the meek alone should be the lords of the earth can be fulfilled only through a complete revolution and a removal of all injustice and all forces. In other words, it can happen through the establishment of the all-inclusive rule of God over the world.[194]

According to Stephen Rose, Rosemary Radford Ruether "is one of the few bona fide theologians." Ruether said, "The function of the Kingdom is not to literally come but to keep us from stopping where we are. History does not solve this basic dilemma of human existence, but simply reveals it on progressively new levels."[195] In another chapter, she said, "Such a struggle, even in its failure and disappointment, is recollected as a time of fellowship, commitment, and ecstatic hopefulness as the highest point of living … In such a time of struggle, one feels closest to one's brother … The messianic brotherhood is then the root of the true church, and in its life, one finds the present 'foretaste of the Kingdom of God' and the 'first fruits' of the resurrection. It is in this form that men experience the revolutionary vision. One lays hold of this vision as the deepest moral certitude of one's life."[196]

Anthony Whilhelm said, "He begins with eight beatitudes, the way to the true happiness" (Mt 3:3–12). In this kingdom, the poor, humble, oppressed, and the little people are the happy ones. This is a complete reversal of the world's usual standards where the rich and powerful are the favored ones. Everyone who has experienced injustices and looked to God for a better life knows what Jesus was talking about."[197]

Leonard Boff said, "The incarnation of Jesus does not simply mean that God made himself man. It means much more. He really participated in our human condition and took on our deepest longings. He used our language, heavily laden with ideological content … as was the idea of the Kingdom of God. But he tried to give our language a new meaning of total liberation and absolute hope. He demonstrated this new content with typical signs and actions. The Kingdom of God that he preached is no longer an unattainable human utopia … it is already initiated in our world."[198]

G. Eldon Ladd said, "We have found that the Kingdom of God is God's redemptive reign. It is God's conquest through the person of Christ over His enemies: sin, Satan, and death. God's Kingdom is manifested in several great acts. At the Second Coming, His Kingdom will appear in power and glory. But this glorious Kingdom of God, which will be manifested at Christ's return, has already entered into history, but without the outward glory. The future invaded the present. The Kingdom of God which is yet to come in power and in glory has already come in a secret and hidden form to work among men and within them."[199]

Gerald Sorin said, "Most important of all, evangelism gave fresh meaning to the lives of many Christian men who were troubled by a changing and materialistic world. It was a practical faith which saw sin in worldly, concrete terms—in evil actions and oppressive institution; it builds in its converts a present obligation to fight sin; and it optimistically predicted the abolition of sin as a giant step toward the building of God's Kingdom on earth."[200]

The Kingdom of God is not only about struggle for the illumination of the power of darkness and evil which end there—it is a continuous struggle for a relationship with God. We should learn from the highly recognized New Testament scholar, Bruce Manning Metzger.

In short, the kingdom of God as it is presented in the teaching and work of Jesus is essentially God's sovereign reign. It begins in the personal relationship between God as king and men as subjects. Though in establishing this relationship God takes the initiative, human effort is not lacking: "Seek his kingdom … for it is your Father's good pleasure to give you the kingdom" (Luke 12:31–32). Not everyone who says "Lord, Lord" will enter the kingdom, but he who does the will of the God (Mt 7:21). In other words, to be in the kingdom presupposes a relationship of obedience to God.[201]

Conclusion

Lessons from our historical experiences, particularly the nationalistic Church like IFI, are enlightening witnesses for learning and understanding the human response to his historical situation—political, social, and ecclesial. Our grasp of human behavior displayed in *history* is one important instrument to our honest desire to effectively respond to the call for pro-human and pro-life mission of the Church of Christ toward building up the global relationship among all people of all nations in the world that God loved. As the purpose of this book, the hope is that we named names enough—the kind of political desire and actions and the kind of Churches that it brought; for the good purpose to identify the challenges and roadblocks to the vision of global community of humans to realize the depth of *fraternal* concept anchored to the love of God for His children that we should celebrate in ecclesial *catholicity* of people and life, in which the cause of IFI and its witness to catholicity must not be silenced.

Our hope is to go deeper and be in our ecclesial nature in Godly vision and mission for fraternal relationship among all people under His fatherhood; this is not a new realization of a new church, but economic imperialism overpowered the concept of "brotherhood of all people." As we are in today's world of wars and death of many innocent people, uncertainty of life situations, the historical and nationalistic Churches have already lifted up high the Answer, the message of God's love and His Kingdom. That is if not ignored, we are advancing in the kingship of the Prince of peace and the Lord of justice.

We were brought to this situation now, we must say—only the God who loved the world inclusively has the right motive to be global, and no one that honestly identified himself with Him (beyond dogmatism) is an outsider from that very purpose. In the world of ruinous darkness offensive to life, the children of light have no choice but to be global among others in pronouncing God's love, righteousness, and justice. Where chaos is planted by man, Christians must beat the drum for the source of peace.

IFI's historical sense is a gift-revelation of human engagement dictated by the heartbeat of human nature. Unless one is deceived and forced to be detached from his world and reality, historical sense is not a valued *agent* for the kind of community we should build. But man's capacity to see the idea of God's peace (Shalom) is built-in ability reflective of God's image and His likeness. We saw *equality* therefore, recognizing the darkness of *inequality* done by the "lovers of themselves" will never be obsolete in building the global community. Thomas Jefferson, Emilio Jacinto and IFI's initial idea of equality is one wisdom of the honest human. What is being displayed in man's assertion is the manifestation of God's image and likeness in man that saw the broad concept of life-sustaining against the opposite. What is being put in historic advocacy and action in obeying the moral law therefore, as *history* --is God's history, History (reflected in historic man).

When *history* of the people in their struggle for life, justice, and fairness is ignored and treated as if it *does not count* anymore as a "useless" agent for understanding the human and social behavior, we have eliminated the right place to avoid repetition of devilish, ruinous, deathful tendency against life. If history is treated as *nothing* but the names of people and dates, we shut off our interest of understanding the human feelings and heart engaging the issue of justice and respect for human dignity. If history is not valued, we have eliminated the right *venue* to ask questions about life and the right reason to evaluate our conduct and global interest for the interest of lasting peace. If we don't look back because what matters is how we can exploit the situation for materialist and consumerist interests, there, we have eliminated the right place by hiding the actual truth and facts of life from making sense of our Christian beliefs. In the kingdom of deception and lies, the *truth* hurts. If we throw out the absolute fact of humans in history, we are throwing out the absolute instrument to evaluate and understand life. Christians that beat the drum for market-driven and gaining the world are caught up in making Bible doctrines and dogmas and other religious isms or play to get God out of the way for the "omnipotent" imperialists of the world. Here, Church, Christianity, and catholicity must be rescued.

Unless people's history is the basis of making sense of our Christian belief, Churches like nationalistic IFI or Anglican/ Episcopal will remain significant, and the love and brotherhood teachings of Jesus will remain important truth for life. There is no lasting peace, but rather building to hate—in oppressor and oppressed, superior and inferior relationship—until we grasp the wisdom of God that should shape our lives. Pro-commercial imperialists didn't come and go to people's nations without destroying the established culture that is friendly to earth and creatures. Consumerist culture brought by commercial imperialism is planting the spirit or addiction dependency to product consuming in which lifestyle or consumerist standards—the earth seems not to be able to handle it!

Restoration is still doable in Jesus. We still have the ability to identify and recognize the scheme of the enemy of life, and so *change*. In Christ, we can reverse our selfish appetite toward tapping the ability of the human (us and others) to love, reversing the course of hate and death. We are in the situation that we must have the ability to see Jesus' "humility" as the real greatness after we saw our concept of "greatness" that builds darkness, insecurity, and death. We must recognize that we seem to have embraced the temptation of Satan about self, wealth, position, prestige, and power—only to realize that we need to embrace the wisdom of Jesus for life and people. We hear people shouting today about "freedom and democracy" because the culture of selfish dictatorship and (personal or global) selfish empire is seen as not right—we must be true to our democracy by that. We must learn to recognize the Lord of life/people we should serve. In the spirit of Christianity, we shine to reflect Christ's Light in advancing the Kingship of God in the here and now of all humans regardless of race or color—for we are all created equal in the eyes of God.

****

Prayer for the Unity of God's People

O God, the Father of our Lord Jesus Christ, our only Savior, the Prince of Peace; Give us grace seriously to lay to heart the dangers we are in by our unhappy divisions. Take away all hatred and prejudice, and whatsoever else may hinder us from godly union and concord: that as there is but one Body and one Spirit, and one hope of our calling, one Lord, one Faith, one Baptism, one God and Father of us all, so we may be all of one heart and of one faith and charity, and may with one mind and one mouth glorify thee; through Jesus Christ our Lord. *Amen.* [From *The Filipino Ritual*, Iglesia Filipina Independiente; page 31]

End Notes

1   *St. Augustine: City of God,* Gerald G. Walsh, S.J., et.al. Trans., (New York: Image Book/Doubleday; 1958), 229.
2   Jeanne Boydston, et.al; *Making A Nation: The United States and Its People, Volume Two*; (New Jersey: Prentice Hall, 2002), 588.
3   *Saint Augustine: City of God;* 231.
4   Teodoro A. Agoncillo; *History of the Filipino People*, Eight Ed.; (Quezon City: Garotech Publishing; 1990), 232
5   IFI Fundamental Epistle VI, 1902
6   IFI Fundamental Epistle I, 1902
7   Pedro Gagelonia, *The Filipino Historian*, 164
8   Renato Constantino, *Dissent and Counter-Consciousness*, 69
9   John E. Booty; *The Church in History;* (USA: Seabury Press, Inc.; 1979), 3.
10 Ibid.
11 Dr. Manolo Vaño, letter to Bp. Vic Esclamado, May 8, 1993. See Renato Constantino, *The Philippines: A Past Revisited*, 292
12 Renato Constantino, *The Philippines: A Past Revisited (Pre-Spanish-1941), Vol.1,* (Manila: Renato Constantino; 1975), 254.
13 T. Agoncillo; *History of the Filipino people,* 232.
14 Shared thoughts to Bp. Delfin Callao Sr. by activists and Roman Catholic nuns in Butuan City, Philippines.
15 Kenneth Scott Latourette, *A History of Christianity Volume II: A.D. 1500-A.D. 1975,* (USA: Harper San Fracisco, 1975), 1445
16 *St. Augustine: City of God,* G. G.Walsh, et.al. Trans., (New York: Image Book, Double Day), 229.

17 Gregorio F. Zaide, *Philippine History,* (Updated Edition); (Philippines: National Book Store, 1984), 35.

18 Luis H. Francia, *A History of the Philippines: From Indios Bravos to Filipinos;* (New York: The Overlook Press, 2010), 28.

19 Ambrosio Manaligod; *Early Secular Clergy in the Philippines,* 11.

20 Luis H. Francia, *A History of the Philippines: From Indios Bravos to Filipinos;* 65–66.

21 Ibid.

22 Ibid., 66–67.

23 Ibid., 67.

24 Ibid., 69–71.

25 Ibid., 72.

26 Ambrosio M. Manaligod; *Gregorio Aglipay: Hero or Villain;* (Manila: Foundation Book, Communication Foundation for Asia (CFA); 1977), 25.

27 Ibid., 26.

28 Pamphlet by William Henry Scott, "The Philippine Independent Church in History" (Sagada, Mountain Province, Philippines; August 24, 1960).

29 T. Agoncillo, *History of Filipino People,* 122.

30 Gregorio F. Zaide; *Philippine History,* Updated Edition, (Metro Manila, Philippines: National Book Store; 1982, 1984), 59.

31 Renato Constantino, *The Philippines: A Past Revisited (Pre-Spanish-1941), Vol.1,* (Manila: Renato Constantino; 1975), 292.

32 See Gregorio Zaide, *Philippine History,* 59, 106.

33 T. Agoncillo, *History of Filipino People,* 114.

34 Gregorio Zaide … 153.

35 Letter of Manolo Vaño to Bp. Vic Esclamado.

36 T. Agoncillo, *Filipino Nationalism 1872–1970;* 237.

37 Ibid., 124-125; Gregorio Zaide, Pilippine History, 143

38 Ibid., 132

39 T. Agoncillo, *Filipino Nationalism,* 185

40 Dr. Manolo Vaño, *Light in Rizal's Death Cell,* 15

41 Various Translations of IFI.

42 Agoncillo, *History of Filipino People,* 102.

43 Gregorio Zaide, *Philippine History,* 106.

44 Ibid., 107–110.

45 Ibid., 107–112.

46 Various Translation of IFI.

47 T. Agoncillo, *History of Filipino People,* 162.

48 Epifanio do los Santos; *The Revolutionist*, 182.
49 Ibid.
50 T. Agoncillo; *Filipino Nationalism*, 237.
51 J. Herbert Kane, *Understanding Christian Mission*, 257.
52 De los Santos, *The Revolutionist*, 23.
53 T. Agoncillo, *Filipino Nationalism*, 207.
54 Ibid.
55 Ibid., 215.
56 Ibid., 225.
57 John A. Garraty; *The American Nation: A History of United States Since 1865, Vol. Two, Eighth Ed.*, (USA: Harper Collins College Pub.; 1995), 605.
58 T. Agoncillo, *Introduction to Filipino History*, 232.
59 Ibid., 200.
60 Various Translation of IFI.
61 William Henry Scott, "The Philippine Independent Church in History."
62 Luzviminda Fracisco, "The First Vietnam: The Philippine-American war, 1899–1902", Daniel B. Schiemen and Stephen Rosskamm Shalom, Editors; *The Philippine Readers*, 9.
63 Howard Zinn, *People's History of the United States,* 312.
64 Ibid., See also: Howard Zinn, Mike Konopacki, Paul Buhle, *A People's History of American Empire (A Graphic Adaptation)*, (New York: Metropolitan Books, 2008), 65.
65 Zinn, *A People's History of U.S. 1492–Present*, 314.
66 Ibid.
67 Walter LaFeber; *The New Empire: An Interpretaton of American Expansion 1860–1898*; (Ithaca & London: Cornell University Press; 1963), 329. In the book cover stated of it "Beveridge Award-winning study."
68 Ibid., 331.
69 Ibid.
70 Ibid., 332.
71 Ibid.
72 Ibid.
73 L. Joanne Buggly et.al; *America! America!*, 541.
74 *The World Book Encyclopedia: M Volume 13*, 107.
75 Buggly et.al; *America! America!*, 541.
76 Louis B. Wright, et.al., *The Democratic Experience (Revised): A Short American History*, 319.

77 Jeanne Boydston, et.al. *Making A Nation: The United State and its People*, 588.

78 Richard D. Heffner, Alexander Heffner, *A Documentary History of the U.S.*, (New York: A Signet Book, 2009), 287.

79 Davidson, et.al, *Nation of Nations: A Concise Narrative of the American Republic Since 1865*, Vol. Two, Third Edition, (New York: McGraw Hill Companies Inc., 2002), 597.

80 Ibid.

81 Joseph R. Conlin, *The American Past: A Survey of American History*, Fourth Ed., (Forth Worth: The Hardcourt Press, 1993), 538.

82 John M. Blum, et al; *The National Experience: A History of the United States Since 1865*, Sixth Ed.; (USA: Harcourt Brace Jovanovich, Pub. ___), 527.

83 Ibid.

84 Ibid.

85 Joseph R. Conlin; *The American Past: A Survey of American History*, Fourth Ed., (USA: The Harcourt Press; 1993), 238–9.

86 Sidney Fine, "Laissez-Faire and the Businessman," *Pattern In American History*, 39.

87 Ibid.

88 Ibid.

89 Ibid. 39-40. (See Susan Jacoby's *The Age of American Unreason*; New York: Pantheon Books; 2008), 72–73.

90 Ibid.

91 Ibid.

92 Ibid.

93 Louis Snyder, "The Communist Manifesto," *Great Turning Points in History: 25 Events That Changed the World*, (New York: Barnes and Noble Books, 1971), 99.

94 S. Fine, "Laissez-Faire and the Businessman," *Pattern in American History*, 39.

95 Richard Heffner with Alexander Heffner, *A Documentary History of the U.S.*, (USA: A Signet Book, 2009), 217.

96 Kristin L. Hoganson; "Male Degeneracy and the Allure of the Philippines (1998)."

97 *Mark Twain: Tales, Speeches, Essays, and Sketches*, (New York: Penguin Group), 279.

98 Steven M. Gillon, et.al; *History 102: College of Southern Nevada*; (USA: Cengage Learning; 2008); 806.

99   Davidson, et.al., *Nation of Nation: A Concise Narrative of the American Republic,* 606.

100 Nash, et.al; *The American People (Creating a Nation and a Society)*; (New York: Longman; 2001), 646.

101 Jack Estrin, *American History Made Simple,* 123.

102 Augustine, *Confessions,* (New York: Penguin Books, 1994), 146.

103 Alan Brinkley, *American History: A Survey since 1865,* Vol. II; 9th Ed., (New York: McGraw-Hill, Inc., 1995), 564.

104 Garry Nash, et.al, *The American People: Creating A Nation and Society From 1865,* Vol. Two, Fifth Ed., (New York: Eddison, Wesley, Longman Educational Pub., 2001), 645.

105 L. Joanne Buggly, et.al., *America! America!,* 544; see Mark Twain's "To the Person Sitting in Darkness."

106 John M. Blum et.al; *The National Experience: History of the U.S. since 1865*; 6th Edition, 537.

107 Nash, et.al; *The American People.,* 646.

108 H. Zinn, *People's History of U.S.,* 307.

109 Patrick J. Buchanan, *A Republic, Not An Empire: Reclaiming America's Destiny,* (Washington D.C.: Regenery Pub., Inc., 1999), 159.

110 Beard and Bagley; *The History of American People*; 552.

111 Thomas Bailey, David Kennedy, *The American Spirit,* Vol. 2, Sixth Ed., (Massachusetts: D.C. Health and Company, 1987), 154.

112 James Roark, et.al. *The American Promises: A History of the US from 1865,* 3rd Ed., Vol. II, 741.

113 Nash, et.al; *The American People.* 646. See Carol Berkin, et.al; *A History of the Unite States: American Voices*; (USA: Harper Collins Publisher; 1992), 392.

114 John M. Blum et.al; *The National Experience: History of the U.S. since 1865*; 6th Ed., 138.

115 T. Agoncillo, *Filipino Nationalism,* 237.

116 Richard Heffner with Alexander Heffner, *A Documentary History of the U.S.,* (USA: A Signet Book, 2009), 217; see also Bible: Matthew 6:24 NKJV.

117 L. Joanne Buggly, *America! America!*; 536–537.

118 Various Translation of the IFI

119 Apolonio Ranche, "Iglesia Filipina Independiente History: The Founding of the Iglesia Filipina Independiente," *Souvenir Program: 93rd IFI Foundation Anniversary 1995.*

120 T. Agoncillo, *History of Filipino People,* 237.

121 Ibid.

122 Achutegui, S.J., *Filipino Heritage*, 2325.

123 Rebert Broderick, Ed., *The Catholic Encyclopedia*, Revised and Updated Edition., (New York: Thomas Nelson Publishers, 1987), 28.

124 Pedro Gagelonia, *The Filipino Historians*, 164

125 William H.Scott, *Aglipay Before Aglipayanism*, 40.

126 Various Translations of IFI.

127 R.Cruz *Philippine Social Science*, 211.

128 Various Translations of IFI.

129 Fundamental Epistle (of IFI), VI.

130 Ibid.

131 Fundamental Epistle II; see h//www.ifi/ph/Epistle htm; also in "Doctrine and Constitutional Rules of the PIC, 1903."

132 From IFI, Paco Parish, "Misa Balintawak" (Katapusan), (Cantor's file); see also *Imnaryong Pilipino (IP)*, "Misa Balintawak" (Katapusan).

133 Ibid.

134 Rev. Dr. Fred Vergara, *Mainstreaming*, 161.

135 *http://www.ifi.ph/ecumen.htm*. *The Living Church*, "Anglicans Global Mission," January 2, 2011.

136 Booty, *The Church in History*, 177.

137 *Grolier Encyclopedia of Knowledge.*

138 *St. Augustine: City of God*, Trans. Gerald G. Walsh, et.al, (New York: Image Book, Doubleday, 1958), 229.

139 Ibid, 231.

140 Xavier Leon-Dufour (Ed.), *Dictionary of Biblical Theology*, (Philippines: St. Paul's publications, 1968), 308.

141 Richard Dawkins, *The God Delusion*, (Boston: Mariner Books, 2006), 305.

142 See *Catholic Encyclopedia*, "Aglipay Schism."

143 Patrick J. Buchanan, *A Republic, Not an Empire (Reclaiming America's Destiny)*, (USA: Regnery Publishing, Inc.; 1999), 159.

144 Lee Strobel; *The Case for Faith*, 200.

145 *Time*, June 7, 2010; Jeff Israely and Howard Chua-Eoan, "Why Being Pope Means Never Having to Say You're Sorry."

146 Paul Jacob, et.al, *To Serve the Devil: Colonial and Sojourners, (A Documentary Analysis)*, Vol. 2, 137.

147 *Matthew Henry's Commentary on the Whole Bible: Complete and Unabridged*, (USA: Hendrickson Publishers, 1997), 1832.

148 Mel White; *Religion Gone Bad (The Hidden Dangers of the Christian Right)*; (New York: J. P. Tarcher/Penguin; 2006), 60.

149 Richard Dawkins, *The God Delusion* (2006), 329.

150 Anita Miller (editor), *George W. Bush versus the U.S. Constitution: The downing street memos and deception, manipulation, torture, retribution, and cover-ups in the Iraq war and illegal domestic spying*; (Academy Chicago Pub. 2006), xv.

151 Ibid., 5.

152 Ibid.

153 Read it also from their new CD's inside cover; and hear it from the lyrics of the song "Let's Impeach the President." *CD/Album* name is: "CSNY/Déjà vu LIVE; 2008.

154 Greg Mitchell, Editor, *So Wrong For So Long (How The Press, The Pundits—And The President—Failed On Iraq)*; (New York/London: Union Square Press, 2008), 157.

155 Dilip Hiro; *Secrets and Lies: Operation "Iraqi Freedom" And After a Prelude to the Fall of U.S. Power in the Middle East?* (New York: Nation Book; 2004), 1.

156 Dave Lindorff and Barbara Olshansky; *The Case For Impeachment: The Legal Argument for Removing President George W. Bush from Office*; (New York: St. Martin's Press; 2006).

157 John Judis; *The Folly of Empire: What George W. Bush Could learn from Theodore Roosevelt and Woodrow Wilson*, (New York: Scribner, 2004), 2.

158 Ibid., 67.

159 See D. R. McConnell; *A Different Gospel (A Historical and Biblical Analysis of the Modern Faith Movement)*; Updated Edition, 4th printing, 2007, (Massachusetts: Hendrickson Pub., 1988), 11.

160 Ibid.; More books about it: A. Michael Horton, Ed; *The Agony of Deceit*; Chicago: Moody Press; 1990. Walter Martin; *The Kingdom of the Cults*; Minnesota: Bethany House Pub. 1985. Hank Hanegraaff; *Christianity in Crisis*; Oregon: Harvest House Pub., 1993. Dave Hunt & McMahon; *The Seduction of Christianity*; Oregon: Harvest; 1985.

161 Ibid.

162 Manfred T. Brauch, *Abusing Scripture: The consequences of misreading the bible*; (Illinois: InterVarsity Press, 2009), p.69

163 Michael Horton (editor); *The Agony of Deceit (What Some TV Preachers are Really Teaching);* (Chicago: Moody Press; 1990), 43.

164 Ibid., 118.

165 Ibid., 44.
166 Ibid., 119.
167 Ibid., 92.
168 Ibid., 14.
169 Ibid., 112.
170 Ibid., 90.
171 Ibid., 45.
172 Ibid., 90.
173 Ibid., 91.
174 Ibid., 113.
175 Ed Decker, *Decker's Complete Handbook on Mormonism*, (USA: Harvest House; 1995); 283.
176 Ed Decker and Dave Hunt; *The God Makers (A Shocking Expose of What the Mormon Church Really Believes)*; Oregon: Harvest House Pub.; 1984); *See also* the whole chapter 13 page 177-193
177 *Chart*: "Christianity, Cults & Religions'; (California: RW Research, Inc.; 2005).
178 See Jack Rogers, *Jesus, the Bible, and Homosexuality: Explode the Myths, Heal the Church*, (Kentucky: Westminster John Knox Press, 2006), 70
179 Eric Gritsch, *Born Againism: Perspectives on a Movement*; (Philadelphia: Fortress Press; 1982), 9.
180 Randall Balmer; *Thy Kingdom Come: An Evangelical's Lament*, 148.
181 Ibid.
182 Thomas C. Oden; *Agenda for Theology*, 57–58.
183 George Eldon Ladd; *The New Testament and Criticism*, 7.
184 Allan J. Lichman; *White Protestant Nation: The Rise of American Conservative Movement*; (New York: Atlantic Monthly Press; 2008), 26.
185 Eric W. Gritsch; *Born Againism: Perspectives on a Movement*, (Philadelphia: Fortress Press, 1982), 39.
186 Ibid.
187 Ibid., 40
188 Ibid.
189 Pat Robertson, *The Secrete Kingdom*, 16.
190 Peter Wagner, *How to Have Healing Ministry*, 96.
191 Charles Swindoll Radio; Bakersfield, CA. 11.80, "Insight for Living"; Sept. 6, 200_

192 Rt. Rev. Peter Hall, *Decide for Peace*, 26.

193 John Wavoord, Roy Zuck, Editors, *The Bible Knowledge Commentary (An Exposition of the Scriptures by Dallas Seminary Faculty New Testament Ed.)*, 257.

194 George Eldon Ladd, *Crucial Questions About the Kingdom of God*, 67.

195 Rosemary Radford Ruether, *Radical Kingdom*, 129–130.

196 Ibid., 288.

197 Anthony Wilhelm, *Christ Among Us*, 72.

198 Leonard Boof, *Jesus Christ Liberator*, 61.

199 George Eldon Ladd, *Gospel of the Kingdom*, 95.

200 Gerald Sorin, *Abolisionism: A New Perspective*, 47.

201 Bruce Manning Metzger, *The New Testament: Its Background, Growth, And Content*, (Nashville: Abingdon Press, 1993), 149.